Guyon's

SPIRITUAL

LETTERS

D1715304

Madame
Guyon's
SPIRITUAL
LETTERS

 Christian Books Publishing House

Other books by Jeanne Guyon

Experiencing the Depths
of Jesus Christ

Union With God

Song of Songs

CONTENTS

Introduction

Introduction

I recently visited France and there traced the footsteps of Jeanne Guyon's nearly 70 years of life. As I reflect on where this compilation of her writings was penned, the thought fills me with awe. Whatever else might be said of this woman, she led a very dramatic life.

Some of her writings were penned from her home in Paris, others were written in Switzerland. Some resulted from experiences she had while under house arrest in a convent; other writings may have been penned from St. Cyr at the height of her popularity. It is possible a few were written from the dungeon of Vincennes; one letter written during a period of incarceration was even written in her own blood. (Although this letter exists today in the Archives of Paris, it is virtually unreadable.) It is doubtful that any of her correspondence written from the Bastille survived.

Her letters were written to the great, the near great, the obscure and the unknown. Some of her writings are vague, a few defy understanding, some are clear and some lift you to the heavens. The contents of a few of her writings can literally curl the hair of an evangelical. She was, first of all, a Roman Catholic. Today she would be amazed to find herself so popular and so well received among non-Catholics.

Many Christians are very curious about how many books Guyon wrote and how many are available.

She wrote her autobiography throughout most of her life up until her imprisonment. It is generally considered to be one of the most arresting autobiographies ever penned by a Christian. It is also difficult for anyone but a Frenchman to follow. Names and places which have no meaning to most readers cause a Frenchman's mouth to drop open. Guyon crossed paths or swords with some of the greatest names of France's golden age.

Her other great work, *Experiencing the Depths of Jesus Christ,* was written in Grenoble, France about 1685. Until this day it remains one of the truly great pieces of Christian literature of all time.

Union with God is a companion edition to *Experiencing the Depths of Jesus Christ.* The place of its authorship is unknown to me. Later she penned *Spiritual Torrents,* probably the least practical of her best known books.

Her work *A Mystical Commentary of the Bible* is very uneven, probably because it was written in haste and in an escalating atmosphere of tension. Some of it is quite beautiful, other parts lack quite a bit. Mostly it communicates how central Christ was in her thoughts.

After Guyon and her writings fell under the wrath of Louis XIV, she wrote a book entitled *Justifications* in which she explained her teachings, proved — at least to her satisfaction — that she was teaching only what Catholic mystics of the past had taught, and even commented on her commentaries. This work was never widely read and has never been translated into English.

Interestingly, she once wrote a pamphlet explaining what she was talking about in *Experiencing the Depths of Jesus Christ.* I have never seen this booklet even in French, nor do I know of its existence. I did not knowingly run across it even in the Archives of Paris.

The poems and letters of Jeanne Guyon span her lifetime. Her poems have always been enjoyed by Christians and a few were even set to music. Her letters, too, were a favorite for perhaps a century.

Personally, I read Guyon because I am stirred and challenged. Her eccentricities I ignore, the categorization of her teachings I leave to scholars (who fare no better than the rest of us in coming to any kind of consensus on the place of her life and teachings in Church history).

I trust you will enjoy these writings and be arrested by a woman who saw Jesus Christ in virtually every circumstance of life.

Gene Edwards

LETTERS OF MADAM GUYON.

REIGN OF CHRIST IN THE HEART

I HAVE read your letter, my dear brother, with great pleasure. It is my highest happiness to see the reign of Jesus Christ extending itself in the hearts of God's people. An external religion has too much usurped the place of the religion of the heart. The ancient saints — Abraham, Isaac, Jacob, Enoch, Job — lived interiorly with God. The reign of Christ on earth is nothing more nor less than the subjection of the whole soul to himself. Alas! the world are opposed to this reign. Many pray, " Thy will be done on earth as it is in Heaven;" but they are unwilling to be crucified to the world, and to their sinful lusts. God designs to bring his children, naturally rebellious, through the desert of crucifixions — through the temptations in the wilderness, into the promised land. But how many rebel, and choose rather to be bond-slaves in Egypt, than suffer the reductions of their sensual appetite.

Since Jesus Christ appeared on earth, there is a general belief that the kingdoms of this world will ultimately be subject to his dominion. But we may ask, who hastens his coming, by now yielding up his own heart to his entire control?

Our Lord imposed no rigorous ceremonies on his disciples. He taught them to enter into the closet; to retire within the heart; to speak but few words; to open their hearts, to receive the descent of the Holy Spirit.

The holy Sabbath has not only an external, but a deeply spiritual meaning. It symbolises the rest of the holy soul, in union with God. Oh! that all Christians might know the coming of Jesus Christ in the soul! Might live in God, and God in them!

God alone knows how much I love you.

TURN FROM SELF TO CHRIST

You are not forgotten, my dear E. God has engraven you on my heart. If you have not consented to the thoughts that have crossed your mind, do not be afflicted on account of them. The examination and dwelling upon these thoughts, brings them again to life. Be on your guard against everything that entangles you in self. God is a Father who bears with the innocent faults of his children, and wipes away the stains they have contracted. The greatest wrong you can do to God is to doubt his love. He regards the simplicity and purity of the intention. It is right to cherish great self-distrust, to realise your weakness and helplessness ; but do not stop here. Confide as much more in God, as you hope less from yourself.

Do not afflict yourself, because you do not at all times realise a *sensible* confidence in God, and other consoling, happy states. Walk by faith, and not by sight, or positive perception of the good you crave. Let us, my dear E., be closely united, and walk together; not according to the way we might choose, but according to the way God chooses for us.

I love you tenderly.

ASSURANCE.

Notwithstanding all that is said to me, my dear M., in opposition to my state, I cannot have one doubt of its reality. There is within me an inward testimony to the truth, so deep, that all the world could not shake it. It is the work of God upon my heart, and partakes of his own immutability. It seems to me that all the difficulties of theologians concerning this state, arise from viewing it, not in the light of divine truth and power, but in the light of the creature. It is true, the creature, in itself, is only weakness and sin; but when it pleases God to new-create the soul, and make it one with himself, it is then transformed into the likeness of Christ.

Who will dare limit the power of God? Who will say that God, whose love is infinite as it is free, cannot give such proofs of love as he pleases, to his creatures?

Has he not the right to love me as he does? Yes, he loves me, and his love is *infinite*. I do not doubt it. And he loves you, too, dear M., in the same manner. This is eternal love manifested,— the heart of God drawn out, — *expressed* towards his creature.

In this state, we understand the mutual secrets of the Lover and the beloved. Who will so deny the truth of the Lord, as to question this? When I hold my beloved in my arms, in vain does one assert, " It is not so,— I am deceived." I smile inwardly and say, " *My beloved is mine and I am his!*" " If we receive the witness of men, how much greater is the witness of God ? "

HUMILITY THE EFFECT OF LOVE.

I ASSURE you, you are very dear to me. I rejoice very much in the progress of your soul. When I speak of progress, it is in descending, not in mounting. As when we charge a vessel, the more ballast we put in, the lower it sinks, so the more love we have in the soul, the lower we are abased in self. The side of the scales which is elevated, is empty; so the soul is elated only when it is void of love. "Love is our weight," says St. Augustine. Let us so charge ourselves with the weight of love, as to bring down self to its just level. Let its depths be manifested by our readiness to bear the cross, the humiliations, the sufferings, which are necessary to the purification of the soul. Our humiliation is our exaltation. "Whosoever is least among you shall be the greatest," says our Lord.

I love you, my dear child, in the love of the Divine Master, who so abased himself by love! Oh! what a weight is love, since it caused so astonishing a fall, from heaven to earth, — from God to man! There is a beautiful passage in the Imitation of Christ, " Love to be unknown." Let us die to all but God.

DIVINE COMMUNICATIONS.

God communicates himself to pure souls, and blesses, through them, other souls, who are in a state of receptivity. All these little rills, which water others, little compared with the fountain from which they flow, have no determinate choice of their own, but are governed by the will of their Lord and Master. The nature of God is communicative. God would cease to be God if he should cease to communicate himself, by love, to the pure soul. As the air rushes to a vacuum, so God fills the soul emptied of self.

The seven blessed spirits around the throne, are those angels who approach nearest to God, and to whom he communicates himself the most abundantly. St. John, perhaps, was better prepared than any of the apostles to receive the Word, incarnate, dwelling in the soul.

On the bosom of Jesus, — in close affinity with him, — John learned the heights and depths of divine love. It was on this account our Lord said to his mother, " seeing the disciple stand by whom he loved, Woman behold thy Son." He knew the loving heart of John would give • her a place in his own home.

God communicates himself to us in proportion as we are prepared to receive him. And in proportion as he diffuses himself in us, we are transformed in him, and bear his image. O, the astonishing depths of God's love! giving *himself* to souls disappropriated of self, becoming their end, and their final principle, their fulness, and their all.

JOY IN PERSECUTIONS.

I am very grateful to you, my dear sir, for your sympathy in my apparent ills. God has not permitted that I should consider them otherwise than blessings. I trust what appears to destroy the truth will, in the end, establish it. Those who maintain the inward reign of the Holy Spirit will yet suffer many persecutions. There is nothing of any value but the love of God, and the accomplishment of his will. This is pure and substantial happiness. This joy no man taketh from us.

It is my only desir to abandon myself into the hands of God, without scruples, without fears, without any agitating thoughts.

Since I am there, O Lord, how can I be otherwise than happy? When divine Love has enfranchised the soul, what power can fetter it? How small the world appears to a heart that God fills with himself! I love thee, my Lord, not only with a sovereign love, but it seems to me I love thee alone, and all creatures only for thy sake. Thou art so much the soul of my soul, and the life of my life, that I have no other life than thine. Let all the world forsake me; my Lord, my Lover lives, and I live in him. This is the deep abyss where I hide myself in these many persecutions. O, abandonment! blessed abandonment! Happy the soul who lives no more in itself, but in God. What can separate my soul from God? Surely, none can pluck me from my Father's hands. All is well, when the soul is in union with him.

LIBERTY IN CHRIST.

"If the Son make ye free, ye shall be free indeed." When the man of sin is destroyed, and the new man established in the soul, it finds itself in perfect liberty. As a bird let loose from its cage, the soul goes forth, unfettered, to dwell in the immensity of God. The natural selfish life restricts the soul at every point; and even God, the great *I am*, is unseen, or deprived of his glory.

When Paul asked, "Who shall deliver me from this body of death?" he added, "I thank God, through Jesus Christ our Lord." That is, when by the grace of God, the new man is established in my soul, I shall be delivered. And, subsequently, when deliverance came, he cried out in transport, "I live, and yet not I. Christ liveth in me!" He was now no

more occupied of himself, but let Jesus
Christ live and act in him; he was animated by him, as the body is of the soul.
If another soul animated our body, the
body would obey this new soul; it would
become the moving-spring of its operations.
Thus Jesus Christ becomes the life of the
new man. And what can be more free,
more enlarged, than the soul of Jesus?
His nature is divine, eternal, boundless.
Alas! to what a narrow point does self
reduce us! Who that looks at the freedom
and expansion of the soul, as it puts on
the new man, Christ Jesus, will not crush
the reptile self to the dust, that the life of
God may again, as in its first creation,
animate the soul?

This liberty is as the eagles' wings, of
which the prophet speaks, which carries
the soul on high. The dove that lighted
on Jesus, was an emblem, not only of
innocence, but of freedom, — of liberty of

spirit to soar and dwell in God. May it please God to give you an experience of this liberty. Quit self, and you will find the freedom and enlargement of the All in All.

MELANCHOLY AVOIDED.

I ASSURE you, my dear M., I sympathize deeply in your sufferings; but I entreat you, give no place to despondency. This is a dangerous temptation,— a refined, not a gross temptation of the adversary. Melancholy contracts and withers the heart, and renders it unfit to receive the impressions of grace. It magnifies and gives a false coloring to objects, and thus renders your burdens too heavy to bear. Your ill-health and the little consolation you have from friends, help to nourish this state. God's designs, regarding you, and his methods of bringing about these designs, are infinitely wise.

There are two methods of serving little children. One is, to give them all they want for present pleasure. Another is, to deny them present pleasure for greater good. God is a wise Father, and chooses the best way to conduct his children.

A sad exterior is more sure to repel than attract to piety. It is necessary to serve God, with a certain joyousness of spirit, with a freedom and openness, which renders it manifest that his yoke is easy; that it is neither a burden nor inconvenience.

If you would please God, be useful to others, and happy yourself, you must renounce this melancholy disposition. It is better to divert your mind with innocent recreations, than to nourish melancholy. When I was a little child, a nephew of my father's, a very godly man, who ended his days by martyrdom, said to me, " It is better to cherish a desire to please God, than a fear of displeasing him." Let the desire to please God, and honor him, by an exterior all sweet, all humble, all cordial and cheerful, arouse and animate your spirit. For this I pray. Ever yours.

GOD'S CARE OF THE SOUL COMMITTED TO HIM.

O, THAT you could realize, my dear friend, how much God loves you. As a painter draws upon his canvas what image pleases him, so God is now preparing your soul, by these inward crucifixions, to draw upon it his own likeness. He cherishes you as the mother her only son. He would have you yield readily to his will, even as the branches of the tree are moved by the light breath of the wind. In proportion to your abandonment to God, he will take care of you. When you yield readily to his will, you will be less embarrassed to discern the movements of God. You will follow them naturally, and be led, as it were, by the providencies of God. God will gently arrest you if you mistake. God has the same right to incline and move the heart

as to possess it. When the soul is per·
fectly yielding, it loses all its own consist·
ency, so to speak, in order to take any
moment the shape that God gives it; as
water takes all the form of the vases in
which it is put, and also all the colors.
Let there be no longer any resistance
in your mind, and your heart will soon
mingle in the ocean of love; you will
float easily, and be at rest.

POWER OF THE ADVERSARY.

I AM deeply afflicted that so many, at
the present day, and even some good persons, allow themselves to be openly seduced
by the Evil One. Has not our Lord
warned us against "false prophets, and
the lying wonders of the *last days?*" All
true prophets have spoken in the name
of the Lord — " *Thus saith the Lord.*"
Nothing gives the enemy greater advan-
tage than the love of extraordinary manifestations. I believe these external movements are a device of the evil one, to
draw away souls from the Word of God,
and from the interior tranquil way of faith.

The tendency of all communications
from God, is to make the soul die to self.
An eminent saint remarks, that she had
often experienced illuminations from the
angel of darkness, more pleasing, more
enticing, than those that came from God.

Those delusory manifestations, however, leave the soul in a disturbed state, while those that come from God humble, tranquilise and establish the soul in Him. The most dangerous seductions are those, which assume the garb of religion and have the semblance of truth.

Elias appeared alone among four hundred prophets of Baal. These prophets were much agitated, attracting great attention, " crying aloud," etc.

When Elias was told by the angel, that he would see the Lord in Mount Horeb, he *hid himself* in a *cave*. He saw a great trembling of the earth. God was not there. There came a great whirlwind. God was not there. Then there came a little zephyr. *God was in the still small voice.*

The only true and safe revelation, is the internal revelation of the Lord Jesus Christ in the soul. " My sheep hear my voice." This involves no disturbance of our freedom, of the natural operations of the mind ; but produces a beautiful harmonious action of all the powers of the soul. I beseech you, my friend, in the name of the Lord, to separate yourself from all these delusions of the adversary.

UNCTION OF GRACE.

FRIDAY morning, the 15th, I suffered very much, on account of *the individual*, whom you know. It seemed to me, that God wished that *the all of self* in him should be destroyed. I perceived, that although the truths he uttered, proceeded from the inward work of the spirit upon his heart, his reasoning faculty operated so powerfully, without his perceiving it, that the effect of these truths was in some degree lost. Souls are won more by the unction of grace — by the weapons of love — than by the power of argument.

Are not the truths you utter, my friend, too much' elaborated by the intellect, and polished by the imagination? Their effect seems to be lost, for want of simplicity and directness. They fall pleasantly on the ear, as a lovely song, but do not reach and move the heart. There is a lack of unction.

Are you not always laboring for something new and original, thus exhibiting your own powers of mind, rather than the simple truth?

Receive this suggestion, and light will be given you upon it. Do I speak too plainly? To speak the truth, and the truth only, is all I desire. I have this morning prayed, rather to be taken out of the world, than to disguise the truth. I have proclaimed it, in its purity, in the great Congregation, and it will be seen that Thou, O Lord, hast distilled it in my heart; or rather, O Sovereign Truth, that Thou art there thyself, to manifest thyself plainly, and that Thou dost make use of weak things to confound the strong. God is truth and love. In Him yours.

SPIRITUAL ONENESS.

My union with you, my dear child, is steadily increasing. I bear you in my heart with a deep and absorbing interest, and seem anxious to communicate to you the abundant grace poured into my own soul. How close, how dear is the union of souls, made one in Christ! Our Savior beautifully expressed it, when he said, " Whosoever shall do the will of my Father, the same is my mother, sister and brother. " There is no union more pure, more strong, than the union of souls in Christ! In this manner, pure as delightful, the saints in Heaven possess each other in God;—a union which does not interrupt the possession of God, although it is distinct from God.

Let your soul have within it, a continual *Yes*. When the heart is in union with God, there is no *Nay*, — it is *Yes, be it so,*

40

which reverberates through the soul. This *Yes*, this suppleness, renders the heart agreeable to the heart of the Spouse. It was thus with Mary, the mother of our Lord, when the angel messenger came to her, she replied, " Behold, the handmaid of the Lord, be it unto me according to thy word. " It was thus with the child-like soul of Samuel, when he said, " Speak, Lord, for thy servant heareth. " It was thus with our divine Lord, " Lo, I come to do thy will. "

Yours in the fellowship of the Saints.

VICISSITUDES IN EXPERIENCE.

As the outgoings of life proceed from the living man, while we live in ourselves, we have a strong will and eager desires, and many fluctuating states. But in proportion as our will passes into the will of God, the desires which are the offspring of the will, are subjugated, and the soul is reduced to unity in God.

As the soul advances in the life of God, its natural or selfish movements decrease; and it depends less on mere emotional exercises, and there is really less *variation* of the emotions.

Rest assured, it is the same God who causes the scarcity and the abundance, the rain and the fair weather. The high and low states, the peaceful and the state of warfare, are each good in their season. These vicissitudes form and mature the interior, as the different seasons compose the year. Each change in your inward experience, or external condition, is a new test, by which to try your faith and love; and will be a help towards perfecting your soul, if you receive it with love and submission.

Leave yourself therefore in the hands of Love. Love is always the same, although it causes you often to change your position. He who prefers one state to another, who loves abundance more than scarcity, when God orders otherwise, loves the gifts of God more than God himself.

God loves you; let this thought equalise all states. Let him do with us as with the waves of the sea, and whether he takes us to his bosom, or casts us upon the sand, that is, leaves us to our own barrenness, all is well.

For myself, I am pleased with all the Lord orders for me. I hold myself ready to suffer, not only imprisonment but death; perils everywhere — perils on the land — perils on the sea — among false brethren; all is good in Him, to whom I am united forever.

PATIENCE WITH THE FAULTS OF OTHERS.

I LOVE you very much, my dear M. If my love could be of any avail, it would console you, for I feel a greater tenderness and sympathy for you, than I am able to express. I am more certain than ever, that God designs you for himself. Live exteriorly with N., as being entirely reconciled. Make not too much account of his coldness, his passionate temper, his contempt. It is not by these you are to regulate your conduct, but by a motive more elevated—God and his glory. Let your heart endure his bitterness, for the love of Him, who preferred grief to pleasure. At the same time, do no violence to your own sacred feelings, to accommodate yourself to him, in order to give him a pleasure he cannot appreciate. Regard your present condition, as a means God has given you, to manifest your love to himself, by a willingness to sacrifice yourself. Reject not this cross, shall I not rather say *crown*, and let all be accomplished between God and your soul, in such a quiet manner, that the struggle with your own feelings will not be perceived.

While you are bearing this daily cross—this real crucifixion — I am certain God will sustain you, from the fulness of his love. All is alike good, when God is with us. I love you tenderly. God loves you; let this make amends for all. In Him devotedly yours.

HOW TO DISTINGUISH THE MOVEMENTS OF GOD.

You enquire, how one who desires to follow the movements of God's spirit, may distinguish these movements, from the natural operations of the mind. There is not, at all times, a positive certainty regarding divine movements. If it were so, we should become infallible as the angels; that is, if we were as pure in our intentions. We must walk with God, in entire abandonment and uncertainty, at the risk of sometimes making mistakes, which in the infancy of experience is unavoidable. He who wishes for a particular inspiration, or direction in common matters, which his own reason and judgment can determine, is liable to deception.

A pure soul acts in simplicity, and without certainty, being persuaded that what is good comes from God, and what is not

good from self. The greater the simplicity,
— the more separate from the mingling of
self-activity — the purer are these operations; because the soul in this state is only
a simple instrument, that the Word, which
is in her, moves, so that it is the Word
which speaks and not herself. This manner of speaking, relates to matters of
importance, and not to the minute concerns
of every-day life. The divine Word, *in all
exigencies*, is found in the soul, that is
wholly consecrated to Christ. " When
they bring you before magistrates and
kings, etc., it shall be given you in *that
hour* what ye shall speak." This method
of divine leading — by t'ie hour and by the
moment — leaves the soul always free and
unencumbered, and ready for the slightest
breath of the Lord. This breath, in the
pure soul, is as the gentle zephyr, and not
as the whirlwind, which shakes the earth.
Do not then expect to have anticipated
movements, or movements beforehand from

God. I have an experience of many years, that God often makes known his will, only in the time of action.

If a pure soul, wholly sacrificed to God, should undertake something contrary to the will of God, it would feel a slight repugnance, and desist at once. If one does not feel this repugnance, let the act be performed in simplicity. A mother who holds her child by a leading-string, loosens it, that it may walk; but if about to make a mis-step, she draws the string. The repugnance which a holy soul feels to do a thing, is as when the mother draws the leading-string.

STATE OF SIMPLICITY.

I EXPERIENCED recently, a marked perception of your state, as one in which God took delight, and upon which he had infinite designs, regarding himself and his glory. I saw clearly the state to which God desired to bring you — the means to be used, and the obstacles in the way — the mutual sympathy and confidence he required between us — and the openness and freedom of communication necessary for our mutual benefit, and that we should not hesitate to speak freely of each other's faults.

The peculiarity you remark in my experience, needs some explanation. You say I do not seem to be wounded, nor blame myself when reproved for a fault. To which I reply simply, there is no more of self remaining in me to be wounded. This indifferent state you notice in me, arises

50

from the state of innocency and infancy in which I find myself. Our Lord holds me so far removed from myself, or from my natural state, that it is impossible for me to take a painful view of myself. When a fault is committed by me, it leaves no traces on the soul; it is as something external, which is easily removed. Do not infer that I am blind to my faults. The light of truth is so subtle and penetrating, that it discovers the slightest fault. Souls which are in the natural life, have real faults, as a paper written over with ink is strongly marked, therefore they see and feel them. But souls, transformed into God, have faults, as a writing traced on sand when the wind is high, the wind defacing it as soon as it is traced. This is the economy of divine wisdom, relating to souls in union and harmony with God. Oh! the greatness and simplicity of the way of Truth! How unlike the world's apprehension of it!

QUENCHING THE SPIRIT

DESIRING to follow closely the divine leading, I expressed to you the other day, some sentiments you were not able to receive. I perceived at once, that on account of your resistance, I could say no more. From this experience, although painful as regards yourself, I learnt the extreme delicacy of the spirit that seeks to aid others; and the strength of man's freedom to oppose this operation. I realized, also, my inability to act of myself; for, as soon as the spirit in me was silent, I had nothing to say. I had, however, the extreme satisfaction of knowing, that this good spirit alone conducted me; and that I would not, in the least degree, add, nor diminish from its operations.

It was from a knowledge, gained by experience, of the extreme delicacy and purity of this divine spirit, that I remarked to you, the other day, that if you did not receive the instructions I then imparted, I should have nothing farther to communicate to you. O, how pure and how unlike the impetuous operation of man's spirit, is this operation of God!

SUFFER THE CRUCIFIXIONS AND REDUCTIONS OF SELF.

ALL the graces of the Christian, spring from the death of self. Let us, then, bear patiently the afflictions, which reduce this overflowing life. There is a suffering in connection with confusions and uncertainties, very trying to bear. Unbounded patience is necessary, to bear not only with ourselves, but with others, whose various tempers and dispositions are not congenial with our own. " Offences," — wounds of spirit will occur while we live in the flesh. These offences must be borne in silence, and thus subjugated and controlled by the spirit of grace. By a law of our nature, we feel, more or less, the influence of the spheres in which we move.

While we honor, we think, the true cross, the affliction that comes from God, let us remember, that these instruments,

54

so disagreeable, are the true cross that providence daily furnishes us.

Do not sully the cross and mar its operations, by your murmurs and reflections. Let us welcome any trials, that teach us what we are, and lead us to renounce ourselves and find our all in God.

Jesus Christ says, " He who renounces not all that he hath, cannot be my disciple." Of all possessions, that of ourselves is the most dangerous.

Please present my cordial regards to your brother. I sympathize deeply in, his misfortunes. I use this expression, in conformity to common usage, but it does not express the sentiments of my heart. I am convinced that the loss of wealth, worldly honor, persecutions, are the best instruments to unite us to Jesus Christ. All evils, or apparent evils, are great blessings when they unite us to our All in All. I pray God to sustain him. His sufferings only increase my sympathy and love for him in our Lord. My health is still feeble, but all is well in the depths of my heart. God is there.

REPROVE IN LOVE.

I<small>T</small> is important to use great care and sweetness in reproving others. Reprove only when alone with the person, and take not your own time, but the moment of God. As we are not free from faults ourselves, we must not expect too much from others. Be yourself very humble and child-like, and this character will act sympathetically on others. Jesus Christ was full of sweetness and charity. How patiently did he bear with his imperfect disciples, even with Judas, without anger, without bitterness, and even without coldness.

How lowly was Jesus! He "did not break the bruised reed." He imparts to his little ones no tyrannic power. They use no violence in dealing with souls, but say with John, "Behold the *Lamb of God,* who taketh away the sins of the world."

Our Lord "rejoiced in spirit," in an unusual manner, such as we find nowhere else in Scripture, when he said, "I thank thee, O Father, Lord of heaven and earth, because thou hast hid these things from the wise and prudent, and revealed them unto *babes*." How happy are we in the presence of a little child; how much at ease! It imposes on us no burden of restraint, of fear, of management! It is in this childlike disposition of meekness, of sweetness, of innocency, that we should seek to benefit others.

In the love of Jesus, yours.

SILENT OPERATION OF GRACE.

I PERCEIVE, by your letter, you are in doubt about the grace which passes interiorly from heart to heart. We notice an illustration of this in the woman who touched our Lord, when he said: " I perceive that virtue is gone out of me." In a similar manner, without words, one heart may communicate grace to another heart, as God imparts grace to the soul. But if the soul is not in a state to receive it, the grace of the interior is not communicated, as is expressed in another passage; " If they are not children of peace, your peace will return to you again." This illustrates, according to my view, pure interior communications of the grace of God, from heart to heart, which the soul relishes in silence, and which silence is often more efficacious than a multitude of words.

At our last interviews I had an inclination for silence, but finding in you an aversion to silent communion, I entered into conversation, but without any interior correspondence on my part, and, evidently, without any benefit to you. God would teach you, my dear child, there is a silence of the soul through which he operates, filling it with the unction of grace, to be diffused on other hearts who are in a state of receptivity, often more efficacious than words to replenish the soul.

We find this still harmonious action in nature. The sun, the moon, and stars, shine in silence. The voice of God is heard in the silence of the soul. The operation of grace is in silence, as it comes from God, and may it not reach and pass from soul to soul without the noise of words? O, that all Christians knew what it means to *keep silence* before the Lord!

LIMIT NOT YOUR SPHERE.

LET me urge you, my child, to enlarge
your heart; or, rather, suffer it to become
enlarged by grace. This contraction shuts
you up in yourself, and hinders an agreeable openness which we should ever maintain, even towards those who have no
particular affinity with ourselves. An
open, frank exterior wins confidence. Let
it not appear, that you have so much relish
for yourself, as not to think of others.
What seems to us a virtue is sometimes
regarded by God as a fault; and which
we shall so perceive, when we have clearer
light.

You seem to mark out for yourself a
certain sphere, and if you go beyond it,
you think you do yourself an injury.
Thus, while you have an apparent movement, you are only describing a circle,
whose centre and circumference is self.

I entreat you, pass beyond the narrow bounds of self;—suffer yourself to be led out of self into the will and way of God. Thus you will be much more happy and useful. If I loved you less, I should be less severe.

Let God be the sovereign Master over our hearts, and instruct, and reprove, and operate in us, by himself, or through others, as pleases him.

Adieu. God bless you, my child.

SECRET OF DIVINE OPERATIONS UPON THE SOUL.

Do not suppose, Dear Sir, that you are to be purified by great trials and extraordinary events. All is accomplished in you by the suppleness of your will, — by the state of infancy. It must be so on account of the pride of your natural reason. God conducts the soul in a way opposed to human philosophy. Hence the necessity of being reduced to the state of infancy, and to the subjection of the will. What we call the *death* of the *will*, is the passage of our will into the will of God. This change implies not only a change in externals, but the inward subjection of the desires and sentiments of the heart. Here most persons, who commence the religious life, stop short. They cannot submit to the interior crucifixion, which lays prostrate the whole of the natural carnal life, and consequently there follows a mingling of the spirit of the flesh with grace, and it is this which produces such monsters in the religious world. Do we not read in Scripture, that in consequence of the alliance of the sons of God with the daughters of men, giants were born, who so filled the earth with wickedness, they drew down a deluge of wrath upon the world? It is from this abominable alliance of the flesh with the spirit, that all those who appear in the world, as " mighty men, men of renown," are produced and sustained. One may be full of the natural life, while apparently dead to the external things of the world. Thus they are dead to inferior things, and alive in the most essential points — dead in name, but not in reality.

By an authority as gentle as efficacious, God accomplishes his will in us, when we have surrendered our souls to him. The consent we give to his operations, and our relish of them, is sweet and sustaining, in

proportion to the perfection of our abandonment. God does not arrest the soul
with violence. He adjusts all things in
such a manner, that we follow him happily,
even across dangerous precipices. So good
is this Divine Master, so well does he
understand the methods of conducting the
soul, that it runs after him, and makes
haste to walk in the path he orders.

Suppleness of soul is, therefore, of vital
consequence to its progress. It is the work
of God to effect this. Happy are the souls,
who yield to his discipline. God renders
the soul, in the commencement, supple to
follow illuminated reason; afterwards to
follow the way of faith. He then conducts
the soul by unknown steps, causing it to
enter into the wisdom of Jesus Christ
which is so different from all its former
experience, that without the testimony of
divine filiation, which remains in the soul
in a manner hidden, and the ease and
liberty the soul finds in this unknown

way, it would consider itself as being separated continually from God, being left, as it were, to act of itself. Human wisdom being here lost, and the powers of the soul controlled by the wisdom of Jesus Christ, born in the soul, it increases in its proportions, even unto the stature of a perfect man in Christ Jesus.

The soul, having now passed into God, is in its proper place, and will be happy, provided it remains fixed and separate from its former manner of acting.

Reason may at times oppose with all its strength, and cause some fears, some hesitations; but, being fixed in God, it is impossible for the soul to change its course ; and, after the experience of many useless sufferings, having their origin in self, it suffers itself to be drawn in the current of love. There is now no more of violence to nature. The soul is in its natural state. The ease and naturalness of this state causes, at times, some fear, some anxiety.

It is as much the nature of man, originally, and in his new creation in the likeness of Christ, to be in God, and to be there in perfect enlargement, simplicity, and innocence, as it is the nature of water to flow in its channel. When man is as he should be, his state is one of infinite ease and without limitations, because he is created sovereign, or master of himself, and cannot be subjected by anything created, although he is subjected to God, if that may be called subjection, which brings the soul into affinity with God, and makes it partaker of his nature.

Be therefore persuaded, that God uses no violence in dealing with the soul. This commotion in the soul, arises from the resistance of man's will to divine operations. When the soul is disenfranchised of all that is opposed to the will of God; when it is not arrested either by desires or repugnancies, it runs without stopping or weariness in the way. This is what is called death,— death to self; but the soul was never so much alive; it now lives the true life, the life of God.

When the soul becomes one with God by the loss of its own will and life, it has purposes, and it is important to follow them; but they are purposes in God, and have in them nothing of self. All that has rapport to self is no more, and God is all. Being passed into God, the soul is changed and transformed in him. This is what the mystics call *Resurrection*. But the word used in this way, does not bear its usual signification. To resuscitate is to revive the former life. But in this case, the will, or natural life is consumed, and gives place to the will or life of God. Thus the Holy Spirit operates effectively in the soul, transforming it into the likeness of the Son of God.

Now the soul participates in the qualities of God, one of which qualities, is that of communicating itself to other souls. Or rather, it is as a stream, which, being lost in a large river, follows the course of the river, communicating itself where the river communicates, watering where it waters, drawing into itself all the smaller rivers, which are destined alike to lose themselves in the great ocean of Love. These streams have no independent life, but proceed from, and flow back into their origin. Here is the consummation of souls in oneness, as Jesus Christ has expressed it, — " *One in us.*" ·

There is divine reality in this truth. Blessed are those who comprehend it! How many walk side by side along these rivers, and yet never mingle their waters! And many there are, also, who haste with eagerness, to precipitate themselves into this divine stream, and flow together, as the souls of the celestial ones, in the fulness of divine love.

This is not a chimera of the fancy ; it is the wonderful economy of divinity. It is the end and object of the creation of the soul — the end and compass of all the efforts of God, regarding his creatures. Here is consummated all the glory, God derives from their existence. All beside are only the means approaching this final end, this glorious termination, and absorption of the soul in Deity. Here is the light which ravishes the soul. A light which does not precede, but follows the soul in its progress; unfolding more and more, as a man in a dark cavern, discovers the concealed places, only when he has remained in it for some time.

This is the pure Theology in which God instructs the angels and the saints. It is the Theology of Experience, that God teaches only to his children, who having abandoned their own wisdom, he has him self become their wisdom and their life. This is the law of wisdom, my friend, for us, — the way of the Lord in us. In him we are one.

NO UNION WITH SELFISH SOULS.

THERE are some souls which cause me great suffering. These are selfish souls, full of compromises, speculations and human arrangements, and desiring others to accommodate themselves to their humors and inclinations. I find myself unable to administer in the least degree to their self-love; and when I would be a little complaisant, a Master, more powerful than myself, restrains me. I cannot give such persons any other place in my heart, than God gives them. I cannot adapt myself to their superficial state, neither respond to their professions of friendship; these are very repulsive to my feelings.

The love which dwells in my heart, is not a natural love, but arises from a depth which rejects, what is not in correspondence with it, or rather what is not in unison with the heart of God. I cannot be with

71

a child without, caressing it, nor with a
child-like soul without a tender attach-
ment. I do not regard the exterior, but
the state of the soul; its affinity and oneness with God. The only perfect union,
is the union of souls in God; such as exists
in heaven, and on earth after the resurrection, life takes effect in the soul.

NEVER YIELD TO DISCOURAGEMENT.

Do not be disheartened, my friend, on account of your slow progress. A long martyrdom is sometimes necessary, in order to purify our souls from the concealed faults of self-love—faults interwoven in our nature, and strengthened by long indulgence. As you cannot control at once the agitations of nature, arm yourself with patience, to accomplish the task little by little; not in the way of direct effort, but rather by ceasing from effort, remaining quiet, permitting neither gestures nor words to betray your feelings.

Could we enter into the highest state of grace, as we enter into a room, it might be easily accomplished. But alas! the door is straight, and there are many deaths to pass; in a word, death to self. It is this long martyrdom, or dying of the old man of sin, which causes all the pains of the interior life. It is rare to find persons, who are willing to die entirely to self, and therefore few reach the highest state of grace.

Have good courage. It is a great work to draw a large ship from her moorings, but when she is in the waters, how easily she rolls! What happiness, when by perseverance, you have triumphed over nature, to find yourself in the abundant waters of grace! I pray God to put his own hand to the work. He will.

In Him, devotedly yours.

WEAKNESS AND IMPERFECTIONS.

WEAKNESS AND IMPERFECTION.

I RECIPROCATE your friendship, madam, with all my heart. Our divine Master knows how happy I am to serve you in any possible way. Oh! madam, it is better to be feeble, when God leaves us in our weakness, than to have a strength which is our own. I once thought, that the pure soul was free from all faults, but I now see otherwise. God clothes his children with frailties, that they may be humble in their own eyes, and be concealed from the eyes of the world. The Tabernacle was covered with the skins of the beasts, while the Temple of Herod was ornamented with gold. Let us not afflict ourselves on account of our littleness and infirmities, since God so orders it, but become as little children. When a little child falls, it cannot raise itself, but lets another do for it all that it needs.

It does not depend on ourselves to make the presence of God more or less sensible. Let the desire for a lively sense of this presence, be crucified to the will of God. Take what is given you. Be as the little child, who eats and sleeps and grows. God gives you the best nourishment, although not always the sweetest to the taste. Adieu! my heart sympathises with you.

ADVANCEMENT.

DURING the process of the soul's purification and advancement, it loses sight not only of itself, but of all things else, except God; and even of the distinct apprehension of our Lord, in his humanity. That is, there are no longer distinct, bounded views and perceptions of Christ, the soul becoming identical with Christ. This is necessary in order to draw the soul into oneness with God. Let all go in the divine order. When the soul has returned to its end and origin, and is lost in God, it finds all it lost, without going out from God.

When the soul is yet in itself, it draws all things to itself, and sees God and all creatures in itself. But when the soul is in oneness with God, it carries all creatures with it in God, and sees nothing separate from God. Seeing all in God, it sees all things in the true light, as with the eye of

God. This is what David calls, "Seeing light in thy light."

May God give you understanding of what I say, and docility and acquiescence in the truths, which he causes to penetrate your soul. I make no reserves, but express freely all my thoughts. The least reserve for self, is as a strong breath against a mirror, it obstructs the view of God. My soul, it seems to me, is clear and transparent, reflecting only what the Master presents; and the execution of his will renders the soul always increasingly pure and transparent. May God be all in all to you

GREATNESS OF SPIRITUAL POVERTY.

Do not measure yourself by others, who may not be led as you are. God chooses to enrich some souls with brilliant gifts, but he has chosen you, stripped of all, in the depths of spiritual poverty. This is the perfect self-renouncement, without which, one cannot be the disciple of the Lord Jesus. All other states, however elevated they may be, are inferior to this pure, naked state of the soul. It is a state, which despoils the lover of all he possesses in favor of his Beloved. It is a state in which the soul is shielded from all inroads of the enemy; who can reach only what remains of self in the creature, and not what is enclosed in God.

God has chosen you for himself alone. You are the sanctuary, which is open only to the high priest, in which is contained the ark of the covenant — the essential will of

God — the sacred place, encompassed by the clouds, where the glory of God appears. Oh! blessed poverty of spirit, in which state the soul is enriched with the best gifts a God can bestow!

Measure not your advancement by relation to the road passed over, but by rapport to the end. There yet remains a great road to pass over, since God himself is the way.

The more fully you enter into his designs, the more I love you.

ASSISTANCE RENDERED BY ONE SOUL TO ANOTHER.

THE interest I feel in your spiritual welfare, my dear F., is very great — so deeply absorbing, that I slept but little during the past night, presenting you in prayer before our Lord. I have an inward conviction, that God is enriching your heart by my humble instrumentality; thus, while he elevates you on one side, he debases you on the other, by communicating his grace through so unworthy a channel as myself. The Spirit has revealed to me your state, when I have received no intelligence from you. God has thus ordered it, for his own glory; and when many years hence, this method of God's operations will be better known — the assistance rendered by one soul to another, without the mediation of the body — the use he has made of this feeble instrument

81

to communicate to you his grace, will serve to substantiate this divine truth and heavenly mode of operation.

There is therefore for you, a means of interior advancement, which no distance of place can interrupt. It will be only from lack of correspondence on your part, that it will be diverted. God desires it, at least for a time, until your soul is entirely in union with himself. This method of communication is only a superior fountain discharging itself into another; or, as two rivers bearing each other to the same sea.

Receive then this poor heart in the fulness of Christ's love, and believe me, no one can be more fully united to you than I am.

SIMPLICITY AND POWER OF THE WORD.

You enquire, my friend, why I do not use obscure terms and extraordinary expressions, in explaining the Scriptures. My Lord teaches me, that while there are no writings so profound as the Gospels, there are none so simple. And further, that simplicity of soul gives simplicity of expression. When we speak of a state beyond our experience, we do so with difficulty, and have recourse to learning to aid us, and use forced expressions.

In the natural, simple expressions of Scripture, there are deep sentiments, adapted to the wants of each soul — to those less and more advanced.

The word of God enters the centre of the soul; it has a penetrating quality; an operative efficiency. No words of man can produce the same effect; at least, none but such as come from souls, who are pure channels of the word of God. It is the good pleasure of our Lord, to express and reproduce himself upon the self-abandoned soul. Who does not admire the profound mystery of the creation of the world, where God produced all things by his word? When God created man, he formed him of the dust of the earth — the lowest form of matter — made of dust, that he might not rob God of his glory! But man thus created, received *the spirit* — the breath of the Word. This dust of the earth became the living breath of God. When Jesus Christ is formed in the soul, he imparts not only a clear understanding of the word, but is himself the Word, reproduced in the soul. Those only in whom Christ dwells, fulfill the word, or have the word accomplished in them. Such only are able fully to interpret the word. It is not learning which best explains the truths of God, but the reproduction of these truths in the life — the experience of them.

FORGETFULNESS OF SELF

I CANNOT compliment you, dear sir, and I am persuaded, that you will expect from me, only the simplicity of the christian. This simplicity leads me to say, only what our Lord gives me. You need more of this simplicity. The frequent self-returns you make, dwelling so much on your unworthiness, although it may have the appearance of humility, is only a refined self-love. True simplicity regards God alone; it has its eye fixed upon him, and is not drawn towards self; and it is as pleased to say humble as great things.

All our uneasy feelings and reflections, arise from self-love, whatever appearance of piety they may assume. The lack of simplicity inflicts many wounds. Go where we will, if we remain in ourselves, we shall carry everywhere our sins and our distresses. If we would live in peace, we must lose sight of self, and rest in the infinite and unchangeable God. These self-returns have a tendency to establish the soul more and more in itself, and hinder it from running into its great original. But it is to this, God is calling you. You withhold from God the only thing he desires — *the possession of your heart.* The time is short; wherefore spend it in the compass and surroundings of self? The single eye sees only God. You act as a person who being called before a king, instead of regarding the king and his benefits, is occupied only with his own dress and appearance. God wishes to disarrange you — to destroy self; and you wish to preserve what he would destroy. Be more afraid of self than of the evil one. It is the spirit of Satan to exalt self above God, and this spirit is fostered by these continual returns you make upon your own doings and misdoings, which leaves no place in your mind for the occupation of God.

DIVERSITY OF MEANS OF SANCTIFICATION.

ALTHOUGH there are impenetrable myste-
ries in God's dealings with souls, in order to
promote their sanctification, it is true that
each soul, aside from the ordinary means,
common to all, has a specific training, and
this method of the divine order can alone
accomplish the work. The means that
sanctifies another may not sanctify you.
You, my friend, will not be led by great
crosses and severe sufferings, but in the
way of helpless infancy. The child-like,
yielding soul is necessary for you; therefore
God has chosen a child, myself, to be your
helper. Forget yourself as the man to
whom many eyes are turned, and become
the little, helpless one, who cannot take care
of itself, but lets another care for it. The
pride, presumption and vanity, of the natural man, must give place to the littleness
and simplicity of the child. Says our

Saviour, " Except ye be converted, and become as little children, ye cannot enter into the kingdom of heaven." O, when shall we learn that it is littleness, and not greatness, that God requires of his child!

God has given me a maternal yearning for your soul. I sympathize deeply in your wants and burdens. Be assured, the eyes of the God of Love are upon you. I entreat you, yield to the influences which are in operation to restore your soul to God. I can offer no apology for my letter; for in all things, I obey my Lord.

COMFORT IN AFFLICTION.

I assure you, Dear Sir, I sympathize deeply in your afflictions. With all my heart I present you before our Lord. I have prayed, and still pray, that if you are called to participate in the sufferings of Jesus Christ, you may partake also of his patience and submission. You will find the Lord at all times near your heart, when you seek him by a simple and sincere desire to do and suffer his will. He will be your support and consolation in this time of trouble, if you go to him, not with fear and agitation of spirit, but with calm, confiding love.

Jesus said to the blind man, whose eyes he anointed with clay, " Go wash in the waters of Siloam " — waters soft and tranquil. O, that you might experience the abiding peace which Christ gives. O, that you might become reduced to the simplicity

89

of the little child! It is the child who approaches the nearest to Jesus Christ. It is the child whom he takes in his arms and carries in his bosom. O, how lovely, how attractive, is child-like simplicity! May the sufferings you are now experiencing, render you, child-like and submissive to all the will of your Father. My ill health forbids my writing more fully. God loves you, and you are very dear to me in him. Amen. Jesus, help.

BEARING FRUIT IN UNION WITH CHRIST.

GOD has united my soul to yours in the oneness of his own nature, and when all the obstructions on your part are removed, you will realize this same divine union. " We have many masters, as said St. Paul, but only *one Father* in *Christ.*" This Father unites himself to us by the impartation of his own nature, and from this communication, of himself to the soul, proceeds our spiritual paternity; or the power by which we communicate to others what we receive from him. We are not always sensible how this power, or aid we render others, is imparted. In some individuals it is more manifest than in others. It always adapts itself to the subject who receives it. All the gifts and graces of the spirit are either more sensible and apparent, or more spiritual and inward, according to the power of receptivity in the individual.

It seems to me that when I am with you, there is only a simple, imperceptible transmission from my soul to yours. You do not perceive any marked results, and they are not great, because you are not in a state to receive much, and often interrupt me by speaking, which causes in me a vacillation of grace. If we were together some considerable time without distraction, you would perceive more marked results. It is the desire of God that there should be, between us, perfect interchange of thoughts, of hearts, of souls; — a flux and reflux, such as there will be when souls are new-created in Christ Jesus. At present, my soul in relation to yours, is as a river which enters into the sea, to draw and invite the smaller river to lose itself also in the sea.

This truth,—the fruitfulness of souls who are in God, whereby they communicate grace, — however much it is rejected, is, nevertheless, a truth. This flux and reflux of communication, like the ebbing and flowing of the great ocean-current, is the secret of the heavenly hierarchy, and makes a communication from superior orders to inferior, — and of equality, between angels of the same order.

During all eternity, the communication of God the Father, and the Son, to angels and saints, and their reciprocal communication to each other, will be a well-spring of blessedness. The design of God, in the creation of men, has been to associate to himself living beings, to whom he could communicate himself. He could create nothing greater than likenesses of himself. All the splendor of angels and saints, is but light reflected from God.

God could not see himself reflected in saints, without their participating of these two qualities, fruitfulness and reciprocal communication. In this life all perfection consists, in that which makes the consummation of this same perfection in heaven

No one can be perfect, if he is not perfect *as* the Father in heaven is perfect; that is, partaking of his nature.

Jesus Christ is the Father of souls; his generation, or the souls that are begotten of him. are eternal in their nature as he is. The figure, " giving us his flesh to eat," is the nourishment he gives the soul in communication with himself; or himself reproduced, or begotten in us. The eternal Word is the essential, undying life of the soul.

DESOLATE STATE.

BELIEVE me, dear madam, I take a deep interest in your spiritual welfare, and 1 earnestly hope your confidence in God will not fail, on account of your present desolate state. As the winter plunges still deeper the roots of the trees in the earth, so the wintry state of the sou. plunges it deeper in humiliation. Remember the confidence of Job, " Although he slay me, I will trust in him." Although stripped of all consolation, and left in the desolation of nothingness, you may yet rejoice in God — out of, and separate from, self. Let the earth be stripped of her foliage; let neither flowers nor fruit appear; yet *God is*, therefore you may be happy. The mother loves to sacrifice herself for her child, and finds her life in what affords it happiness; thus die to self, in relation to God.

When your weaknesses rise up before

you, when you would weep over some error in judgment, or some unguarded expression, do as the little child, who having fallen into the mud, carries its hands to its mother, who cheerfully wipes them, and consoles him after the fall. Can you not believe God loves you, as much as you love the little one enfolded in your arms? Does he not say, " A mother may forget, yet I will never forget thee!"

The discovery of your weakness and emptiness, is an evidence of God's love; and while it is ground for humiliation, it is also of thanksgiving. When it pleases God to fill this void with his grace, it is cause of thankfulness; but if we realized at all times this fullness, we should be in danger of appropriating the grace of God to ourselves. Thus, our times of desolation are necessary, and we should accept them joyfully, as a portion of the bread our father gives us.

Yours in tender sympathy.

SELF-ABANDONMENT.

THE death of self is not accomplished at once. It is for some time a living death. Its opposite, spiritual life, is represented by Ezekiel's vision of the dry bones. First, the bones were rejoined; afterwards covered with sinews; then the flesh appeared; and finally, the spirit of the Lord animated them. When the soul begins to incline towards God, it finds many obstructions; but in proportion as we yield to the will of God, these obstructions are removed. The following simile will help to illustrate my idea. The rivers empty themselves into the sea, before they lose themselves there. Wave by wave following its course, seems to urge onward the river, to lose itself in the sea. God imparts to the soul some waves of pure love, to urge on the soul to himself; but as the river does not lose itself in the sea, until its own waters are exhausted, so the soul reaches God, and loses itself in God, only when the means of supply from self are at an end. As the waves, which are precipitated into the sea, roll many times before they are lost in the sea, so the soul undergoes many changes, before it is received into God.

The results of self-crucifixion are happy, because God then becomes all to the soul. We lose self, and substitute God in its place. We take away the finite, and receive the Infinite. This is blessed.

NO DEPENDENCE ON INSTRUMENTS.

WHAT shall I say regarding the state in which you find yourself, in relation to me? I have no movement either to promote our re-union, or hinder it. Let God direct. Are you leaning upon him, or upon the creature? If on the creature, it is a bruised reed, which will fail you. God sometimes makes use of instruments, whom he finds it necessary afterwards to reject. If he designs to remove me from you, can I have any wish to retain you? God forbid. He may design this separation, to make you die to any confidence in the creature. He may no longer design to use me for your benefit. I might have mingled my own impurity, with his pure light flowing through me. If God permit me to err, it is on account of my pride. I have never given you any assurance of my infallibility. What am I but an erring creature? Leave

me, leave me, and unite yourself only to
God, who will never mislead you. Means
are good, only in the order of God. They
injure us, if we rest in them. If God
remove me from you, acquiesce in his will,
with a devotion worthy of a child of God.
Be humble, and courageous enough to own
your fault, in leaning on an arm of flesh.
Men of the world may be obstinate, but
the child of God should be supple. Whatever separation there may be between us,
believe me, you will always be dear to me
in our dear Lord. I hope, when you are
lost in him, you will find this little drop
of water, (myself) in the same great ocean
of love.

CHILD OF GOD SOON TO DIE.

I HAVE had a presentiment that you would not survive this illness. I lose in you the most faithful, and the only friend on whom I could rely, in the persecutions which threaten me. I feel my loss, but rejoice in your happiness. I could envy you. Death only lends a helping hand to rend away the veil, which hides infinite beauties. Our Lord has strongly cemented our souls. May the benediction of the divine Master rest upon you. Go, blessed soul, and receive the recompense prepared for all those, who are wholly the Lord's. Go, we separate in the name of the Lord; I cannot say a last adieu, for we shall be forever united in him. I hope, in the goodness of God, to be present with you in heart and spirit, at the time of your departure, and to receive with you, the divine Master who is waiting for you. Be my ambassador in the courts above, and say to him I love him.

UNION OF SOULS IN GOD.

THE assurance you give me of the union of your soul with mine, is a great consolation. It is a union to which my heart fully responds, not in a way of emotional transport, but in the depths of peace; there is nothing of nature in it. It is a union in Jesus Christ. We are one in a sense of our lost condition, and one in self-abandonment. Oh! blessed oneness with Christ, where all evils perish; and there remains only the casualities inseparable from the state of humanity. How wonderful is this operation — the sacred mingling of a poor creature with its God, where all the evils of our fallen nature, are removed from the depths of the soul, and the soul, in its elemental being is lost in its original! There all the little ones are united in Him, — these little drops of water reässembled in the divine ocean!

103

How swiftly do the streams embrace each other, and flow into one channel, when the obstructions are removed! When souls become pure in Jesus Christ, they flow into one another with the same rapidity. Purity of soul consists in an entire separation from self, and re-union with God. The soul *can* return to self; it has the power, and therefore is not infallible.

Our union, my dear friend, is independent of the relish or disrelish of all created things and events. You could not be separated from me without being separated from God; for it seems to me, that I am one with him, and inseparable, and you are the same; and thus, we are one in Him, and one with each other.

Ever yours, in the heart of Jesus.

SECRET OPERATIONS OF GRACE.

My heart has been tenderly united to you, during all my bodily sufferings. In proportion as the outward man has been reduced, God seems to be more the life of my soul. Although the operations of God upon your soul may be less marked than formerly, they are no less real. There is a secret fire in your heart, which burns continually, although imperceptibly. This keen and continual operation enfeebles you, because it consumes so rapidly the more sensible and marked operations of the soul. This is, I apprehend, your ordinary state; with occasionally the unction of the oil of grace poured upon the concealed fire, to give you a sweet and clear manifestation of the loving presence of God.

You bear two marked results of the divine presence — interior recollection, and a continual *amen* in your heart; a true and just response to all God's dealings with your soul.

I realise a very close union with you. This union is not in the emotions, and not in the will of man, but in the will of God. It is a union, from which I could no more separate myself, than from God; it is a fulfillment of the prayer of our Lord, " that they may be one, as we are one." It is a union which death cannot interrupt, but will substantiate more and more fully in God.

Ever yours, in our Lord.

TO A YOUNG FRIEND.

You are very dear to me, my child. Do not think I have forgotten you. God alone can render you happy. Give yourself wholly to him, never more to take yourself back. Love him with all your heart. Retire often within the closet of your heart to commune with God. Do not pray to him in a constrained and formal manner, but all simple and natural. God loves better the affectionate language of the heart, than the cold and discursive thoughts of the intellect. The prayer of love softens the heart.

Do not shrink from your ordinary duties. We are often more united to God, in our daily avocations, than in retirement. The reason is, our good Father holds us more closely, when we are most exposed to temptations. Endeavor to maintain, at all times, harmony and oneness with God.

You have only to abandon yourself wholly to divine love, and perform all the duties that devolve upon you. Do not be restive, and thus mar God's beautiful design and operation upon your soul. Place in his bosom of rest, all your inquietudes, and allow him to carry you, as a little child is borne by its mother. This little one has only to regard, lovingly, the smiles of its tender mother.

God will give you a wise discernment as to food and drink, and all the pleasures of life. He calls us to a temperate life, but not to a life too austere. We should avoid the *too much* and the *too little* in eating and drinking.

I pray our divine Lord, to enlighten, strengthen and comfort your heart.

FINAL LETTER TO HER SPIRITUAL GUIDE.

THE state in which I find myself, my Father, takes away from me entirely, the liberty to address you any longer as my Spiritual Guide. I realize so great a detachment from all things, that there remains in me only a triumphant, dominant love, which acknowledges no master but Love. It is my experience, that the closer the union of the soul with God, the more it is separated from all dependence on the creature. I find also, that the secret operations of divine love upon the soul, cannot be expressed. These operations do not consist in sweet and flattering expressions, neither in consolations, in the ordinary way, but in the discovery of mysterious truths; truths, which give so profound a knowledge of God, that the soul can find no language to give expression to these views.

To speak, and to act, is the same thing with God. " He spake, and it was done." When the divine Word operates in the soul, without any obstruction, the soul becomes what this Word wills it should become. When Mary Magdalene was made whole, it was no more Mary Magdalene, but Jesus Christ, who lived in her. St. Paul says, " I live, yet not I, Christ liveth in me." In the same manner, the Word is incorporated into my soul.

Some time since, there was given me a view of the States of Mary, the mother of our Lord. I was alone in my chamber, and my soul was completely filled with divine love. The divine Word seemed to say within me, " I will show thee the chief work of my hands,—a perfect nothing in itself, — the heart of Mary." In this manner was conveyed to me, the inexpressible love of God for men—his operation in pure souls. It was shown me, that her silence and acquiescence in the will of God; her entire self-crucifixion and hidden life were worthy of imitation; and that this same love which had operated so powerfully upon this soul, emptied of self, desired to draw other souls also to her states, and to make an effusion of the same grace and love in them, as in her. O divine love! how great are thy wonders, how marvellous thy operations on human hearts! My soul is lost in the depths of thy secret wonders! Silence, silence — only silence!

I write to you, my Father, for the last time, to bid you a final adieu. I can no longer listen to any other teachings, than this divine Word of eternal Truth, which is spoken in the depths of my heart. But however far separated from you, in the relation of Director, you are very near and dear in the affections of my heart; in that pure love, which is alone the operation of our Lord Jesus Christ.

111

GLORY OF GOD THE ONE DESIRE.

WHAT have we to desire in heaven and on earth, only the glory of God? But it is necessary to desire the glory of God as he desires it. He who has absolute power over the heart of man, has a plan of operations; he does all things in their time; he waits until the hour is come. In coming into the world, our Lord could have converted the world at once, and destroyed all its vices; but the economy of his wisdom did not so direct. When I hear our Lord say, *"Mine hour is not yet come,"* and wishing neither to advance nor retard, for a moment, the hour that his Father had appointed, I am plunged into my nothingness. We are only instruments in his hands, which he may lay aside, or use according to his good pleasure. We should be so dead to self, as to be indifferent, whether he makes use of us or not.

Remain, therefore, my dear friend, in the hand of God. Let him accomplish in you, and by you, all his good pleasure, whether to cast down, or build up. God knows how much I love you.

SPIRITUAL UNION AND AID.

SPIRITUAL union, is a state of the soul very clear in my perception, although I may not be able to give you a definite impression of this state. In order to benefit you, it became necessary for me to enter into your state, to have an experimental knowledge, an endurance and suffering of the same state. By this experience I have been brought into closer relation to God, partaking more fully of the Christ-like nature by being rendered capable of bearing the infirmities of others. And I have had, also, a clearer idea of that quality of God, whereby he multiplies holy souls, by the communication of himself. In this experience, the soul appears to be in God, and God in her, as first cause, drawing and penetrating the soul nearest to himself, and by penetration, in this soul, drawing, through her instrumentality, many other souls.

Although by these powerful rays the soul itself may seem to penetrate and draw other souls, yet it is God who draws them by his efficiency; and he communicates this efficiency, most powerfully, to those in closest contact with himself. So pure and transparent is this soul, that there seems to be no space between the first Mover and the souls moved by the agent or instrumentality. There is a difference between the ray and the body of the sun, although it is difficult to separate the ray from the sun. It is the divine ray, which is transmitted through this soul, as the natural ray through the medium of the atmosphere. These same rays, transmitted through many souls, and from soul to soul, unite them in one common centre, and thus the bond of filiation is complete in God. I may not express myself so as to be understood. May your light supply, what is wanting in clearness of expression

LIVE IN THE PRESENT.

Do not expect, my dear E., that the will
of God will be made apparent to you in
any extraordinary way. The most remarkable events occur naturally. It was by an
order of the Emperor, that Joseph, being
of the house and lineage of David, went to
be taxed at Bethlehem, where the holy
child Jesus was born. The fountain of
water was near to Hagar, when she laid
down the child to die with thirst. Behold
God, my friend, in the present arrangement
of his providence for you, and submit
wisely to passing events. He sees the end
from the beginning, and plans wisely for
his children. O, how good to submit our
limited view to his far sight, reaching
through time and eternity!

Remember, the present moment comes
to you as the moment of God. Use it for
his glory, and every succeeding moment

LIVE IN THE PRESENT.

Thus the present becomes the eternal moment, for which we must render account to God. May God be All in All to us in every passing moment, now and forever.

HOW TO ADMINISTER REPROOF.

A SINGLE word, spoken in the spirit of Christ, with humility and sweetness, will have more weight, in correcting others, than many words uttered in our own spirit. The reason is this: when passion mingles with correction, although the truth may be spoken, Jesus Christ does not coöperate with us. Therefore, the person is not corrected by what we say, but, being opposed to the manner of correction, is more confirmed in the evil. In proportion as Jesus Christ speaks by us, without us, or without the minglings of self, his word is efficacious, and turns the heart of the person to whom we speak, to receive what we say. I know there are some who resist, knowingly, *his* word, but our passionate zeal does not correct them.

It is important to wait the moment of God to correct others. We may see real faults, but the person may not be in a state to profit by being told their faults. It is not wise to give more than one can receive. This is what I call *preceding* the *light*, — the light shines so far in advance of the person, that it does not benefit him. Our Lord said to his apostles, " I have many things to say to you, but you cannot bear them now."

The prophet says, the Lord carries his children in his arms, as a nurse. A nurse could wish that the child could walk alone, but she waits in patience the time. Let us do the same, and never discourage the weak. Let us not destroy the good grain with the tares. Who does not admire ' the long suffering patience of God?" And I may add to St. Paul's words, all unworthy as I am, and of those who admire it, how few imitate it! If those to whom God has given so much grace, have so many faults themselves, with how much patience should they bear with those who are less favored.

BEARING THE STATES OF CHRIST.

DURING my late severe illness, a strong impression rested on my mind, that I was called to participate in the last sufferings of Jesus Christ. The language of my heart was, I am ready, O, Father, to suffer all thy will! In thus yielding my heart, as Abraham when called to sacrifice his beloved Isaac, I realized a new bond of alliance with Christ; and these words, " I will betroth thee unto me forever," was the voice of the Bridegroom to my soul.

When Paul said, " I bear in my body the marks of the Lord Jesus," he did not refer to any external marks in the flesh, but to bearing the states of Jesus Christ. In David are expressed all the states of Christ, with the difference only there is between the type and the original. Job was an eminent instance of being reduced to nothingness, and also of exaltation by the favor of God. Those who pass through the furnace, and suffer with Christ, are prepared to wear the white robe, which adorns the bride, the Lamb's wife. Their souls become the dwelling-place of the Most High.

Are not those beautiful subterranean palaces, which we read of in fable, and which are reached after crossing deep caverns, and so hidden that none can find them, only those to whom the secret is revealed, representative of the interior palace of the soul, where the Lord inhabits; "The king's daughter is all glorious within."

OUR IMPERFECTIONS SHOULD NOT HINDER OUR LABORS FOR OTHERS.

ALTHOUGH I am so weak and unworthy in myself, God uses me for the good of others. The many defects of our temperament, should not hinder our labors in behalf of others. These faults have nothing to do with the grace, which operates effectively on the souls for whom we labor. God reveals himself, through the fathers and mothers in Israel, and thus increases confidence in them; while, at the same time, their weaknesses forbid placing too much dependence on them.

Although our Lord acquaints us with his designs regarding others, and the aid we may render them, yet this should not give us the least desire to aid them, only in the order of his providence. Neither should we be arrested in his work, although the souls we aid repulse the effort. God will make good the results in due time.

It implies great death to self, never to put our hand selfishly to the work of the Lord, as it does, also, never to go a step out of the path in which he leads us. When we mingle self, we retard, rather than advance, his work. Nature is so corrupt that it deeply infests spiritual things, and so subtle as to conceal itself under all artifices.

I do not know why I have written you thus. God knows, and that is sufficient.

DEATH, RESURRECTION.

THIS is no time to be disheartened. When the sinful lusts rebel, leave them to their disorderly cravings. Let them cry, as a child from whom we take away a dangerous yet pleasing toy. Strengthen yourself for crosses and humiliations. You will soon be made alive in Jesus Christ.

The extraordinary peace you have tasted, is the commmencement of the resurrection-life. This peace is not invariable, because the new life is given little by little, yet, I assure you, it will soon fill your whole soul. As God has rapidly advanced inward death, and caused you to run, with a giant step, in the way of self-crucifixion, and this, notwithstanding all the oppositions of the carnal man, he will also thus rapidly advance the resurrection.

The loss, of all things of the earthly life, which follows the recuscitated life, will be deep and extended. The death and burial which precede the resurrection, cannot compare with that total loss, which follows the resuscitated life. This is something different, and in a new state. You will arise from the sepulchre, as the Spouse of the Beloved.

All is consumed in myself, not in the ordinary way, but in a total loss; so that there remains nothing which can be named or known. It seems to me, the death of self is carried almost to infinity, it makes so many unknown steps. Since this morning, this unworthy creature experiences a still greater reduction of self than ever before. Die, live; lose yourself, and find yourself again; then you will have experience of this state.

GRACE DEEPLY INTERIOR.

WHILE you perceive nothing sensible, or apparent, in your religious state, there is, at the same time, evidence to others of a hidden spring of life within your soul. God does not give you the sweet rain which, falling, clothes all the surface of the soul with verdure, but he gives you the deep well-spring, by which means you live and flourish, and produce, not herbs and flowers, which are born and die in the same day, but substantial fruits, ripening for eternity. David said, the life of man upon the earth is as grass, which groweth up in the morning, and withers in the evening. This refers to the natural life, but it is also true of the selfish life of man. It flourishes in the morning of the spiritual life, but no sooner does the sun of righteousness arise in his warmth, than this life withers and is cut down. The righteous

are as a tree planted by the rivers of water,
whose leaf is always green. This is because the roots are well watered by the
deep-flowing current.

God never ceases to operate in your
heart. The calm, resigned state of your
soul is proof of this.

Take good care of your health. Do not
labor beyond your strength. God will
abundantly reward you for your labors of
love in behalf of others. These are labors
he never fails to recompense. I pray God,
my dear F., to preserve you for his work.
I have many things to say, but I forbear.
Your time is precious.

SELF-RENUNCIATION.

God designs you, my friend, for himself but he will lead you by a way, entirely opposed to what you have marked out. He does this in order to destroy your self-love. This is accomplished only by the overthrow of all your purposes, preconceived views, natural reason and sagacity. Self-love has many hiding-places. God alone can search them out. You seek the honor that cometh from man, and love to occupy a high position. God wishes to reduce you to littleness, and poverty of spirit. Believe me, dear sir, you will grow in grace, not by knowledge acquired from books; not from reasonings upon divine truths, but by an efflux from God. This efflux will reach and fill your soul, in proportion as you are emptied of self. You are so much occupied of yourself in speaking, reading and writing, that you give no place to God. Make room, and God will come in.

You speak of your many cares. If you will give yourself wholly to God, these cares will be greatly diminished. God will think for you, and arrange by his Providence, what you cannot effect by long years of planning. In the name of God, I entreat you to renounce your own wisdom, your self-leadings, and yield up yourself to God. Let Him become your wisdom. You will then find the place of rest, you so much need.

May you read this letter, with dependence on the Spirit, which has dictated it, and without regard to the instrument, and your heart will testify to the truth of what I have written. Take courage, and be persuaded that if God destroys the natural life, it is only to give you himself. Endeavor to be nothing, that God may be all. When void, God himself fills the space.

UNEXPECTED FAULTS.

YESTERDAY, after I left the parlor, I uttered some words hastily, and suffered very much in consequence; a suffering not like the pangs of penitence I formerly experienced, but more subtle and interior; and the soul was more acquiescent. Whether it was the words I uttered too precipitately, or the reflections that followed, which caused this suffering, I could not determine. A part of myself seemed to be thrown out of God, as we see the ocean reject certain things, which it receives again more deeply into its bosom. Thus I seemed to myself to be rejected, and without any power to make the least movement to return, and without even a regret that I was rejected. I was willing to remain where God placed me, until the moment he received me again to himself. If I should afflict myself on account of this experience, which was new and unexpected, I believe it would be wrong, and sully still more the soul. The depths of my soul remain unchanged — fixed in God. He removes the impurity, that has exteriorly sullied it, and holds the soul still his own.

APOSTOLIC STATE.

I HAVE read your letter, my dear F., with great pleasure. The true Apostolic state is to become all things to all men; that is, to impart to each one spiritually, according to his necessities. Only those who are reduced to littleness and simplicity, have this power of communicating grace. They have also the ability to sympathise deeply in the states of others; of bearing in some measure their burdens, and are sometimes in great heaviness on their account. This communication of grace and aid, is not necessarily restricted to the personal presence of the individual. We may be " absent in body, yet present in spirit," after the manner of God's operations; and as the angelic powers communicate to us. It is only by the enlightening of God's Spirit, that we realise the state of those to whom we are spiritually united.

Unity of souls is experienced, not only with those in the body, who have affinity with ourselves, but also with those out of the body. I realise with the holy prophet David, a correspondence and unity, which renders our souls one in God. You will experience this unity with the saints more fully, when all perception of self is taken away. St. Paul says, " *Ye are come* to an innumerable *company* of *angels* — to the *spirits of just men made perfect.* " David was in the Old Testament, what Paul was in the New. They were both deeply interior Christians. The Apostles, after having received the Holy Ghost, spake all languages. This has also a spiritual meaning. They communicated grace, according to the necessities of each one. This is speaking the word — the efficacious word, which replenishes the soul. This nourishing, life-giving word is represented by the manna, and the reality is found in the Lord Jesus Christ, who is himself the bread of life in the soul. Amen, Jesus!

PAINFUL EXPERIENCE.

To-day my health is better, and I find myself able to reply to your letter. Let the view of yourself that God gives you be accepted, whether it relates to your fallen condition in general, or to particular faults; but add nothing to this view by your own reflections. These continual reflex acts of the mind do not help you; they do not remove the faults. I am not surprised that you find in yourself so many evils, evils which render you almost insupportable to yourself. When God accomplishes the work of purification, he removes all that is opposed to the divine inflowing life.

These evils of your nature, which are now apparent, and which were deeply concealed, are perceived by you only because they are passing out from their hiding-places. All persons do not have so deep a knowledge of themselves; therefore do not suffer so much, because all are not destined to so profound a death and burial while in the body. Be silent, and drink the bitter cup. These humiliations will endure until your state is in some degree perfected; after which they will become more and more slight, and only at intervals, until the death and burial is consummated.

ECSTACY OF THE MIND, AND THE WILL OR HEART. — THE DIFFERENCE.

THE intellectual part of man can be in some degree united to God; but the soul loses itself in God, only by the loss of the will and by love. This loss of the will is the true ecstasy, which is a permanent state, and is effected without any violence to nature. When love is the controlling exercise, the will follows, and the soul is reduced to unity; as in the natural exercise of love, the stronger the love, the greater the submission of the soul to the object beloved. Sacred love does not bind the soul to a resignation, in some of its parts, but draws it fully, until it is absorbed wholly in this divine oneness.

The mind may tend towards its divine object, with ardor, but the will not concurring, causes dissonance and swooning, or impetuous transports. I call this momentary ecstasy; it cannot long endure without separating the soul from the body.

The difference between these two states is, as that of water, retained in the air by a machine, and of a river, running naturally into the sea, as ordered by the grand Architect of the universe. Love, which carries the will in its train, changes the whole man; this is the divine, the true ecstasy. This is what is called transformation, and loss of the soul in God. It is certain, however, that the creature always remains a being distinct from God.

A VIEW OF SELF.

THE activity of the natural selfish life, is the greatest obstacle to your progress. Allow of nothing which gives sustenance to this life. Be on your guard against applause. Applaud not yourself when you have done well. Admit no reflections in regard to the good you have accomplished, so that all that nourishes self-complacency may die.

Possess your soul in peace as much as possible; not by effort, but by ceasing from effort; by letting go everything that troubles you. Be quiet, that you may settle, as we leave water to settle when agitated. When you discover your errors and sins, do not stop, under whatever good pretext, to remedy them. Rather abandon yourself at once to God, that he may destroy, in you, all that is displeasing to him. I assure you, you are not capable of your-

self, to correct the least fault. Your only
remedy is abandonment to God, and remaining quiet in his hands. If you discovered the depth of inward corruption in
your heart, your courage would fail! On
this account, God conceals from us, in
part, the view of our sins, and discovers
them to us, only as he destroys them.

Rest assured, God loves you. He will
take care of you. Have faith in his love
and mercy. You will see farther by and
by. When you are in trouble, do not fail
to write me. Have good courage, and all
will be well. You are very dear to me in
our Lord.

STATE OF A SOUL IN UNION WITH GOD.

ALTHOUGH, in the latter part of my life, I do not perceive those marked states of abandonment and submission, neither of interior sorrows, such as I formerly experienced, this does not prove that these distinct states no longer exist; but the soul having become more fully established in God, it makes less account of them, or is less affected by external impressions. As pure flowing water leaves no trace where it passes, so these *distinct* states leave no durable impression. The soul seems to have lost its own qualities of resistance and aversion, and runs, without ceasing into its Original. It is on this account I cannot write so fully of my states of mind as formerly. My soul, in its depths, rests in God. " *My peace*, says Christ, *I give unto you.*"

I pray for the church; I mourn at time

that God is so little known and loved ; but these feelings are transient, and the soul is ready to take any impression that God gives it. While it seems to have no consistency of its own, so to speak, it adapts itself to the state of others with wonderful facility. Sometimes even relating amusing stories, to children, and to those who cannot be entertained in any other way.

The soul, in this state of union with God, is sometimes permitted to foretell things to come, which appear very obscure to man, but which are, nevertheless, infallibly true, because proceeding from God. The knowledge of the event, and its full explanation, will come in the fulness of time. The soul is ready for anything; ready for nothing. All that is true comes from God ; what is not true, from the creature. The soul does not seek to justify itself, nor produce humiliation, but passes on, disregarding self, and absorbed in God.

STATE OF REST IN GOD.

IF I do not reply to you, Dear Sir, as soon as you might expect, it is because I hold myself in reserve, until I have a movement to write, and not from any want of regard to you. Relative to the distinct, voluntary acts of resignation, renouncement, it would be difficult, in my present state, to make such acts, because such acts would seem to imply something of self-appropriation still remaining; whereas, I have given to my Sovereign, all that I am; and as far as I know, I have nothing more to give him. My soul is at rest in his will.

It is the same in regard to prayer, or petitions. The soul having a very simple method of prayer, all other prayer seems foreign to it. When it would make a request, and as soon as the soul knows distinctly what it demands, there is something which goes before to accomplish it, without the utterance of words. When the soul utters words, or makes petitions, if the spirit accompanying approves, the prayer is made with ease. If the spirit do not coöperate, the words are uttered with difficulty, or not at all. God takes the place of self in the soul, and there prays for things agreeable to his will. This is a state of the soul, in which it has no desire to originate prayer, but loves to be silent in the presence of God. This is an experience more satisfactory than I am able to express. O, that all the earth knew what it means to keep silence before the Lord!

GREAT HUMILIATIONS.

I HAVE a clear discernment of your state
It seems to me, I see it in some measure
as God sees it; that is, in the pure light
of truth, — the reasons why you suffer, and
the blessed results of these sufferings. I
have known that the period of discipline
would be long, and very long, because you
suffer not only on your own account, but
also for the benefit of others. God destines
you to accomplish great things for his glory,
and exterior humiliations in your case not
being suited to his designs, he makes use
of concealed humiliations, known only to
yourself and God. I will repeat to you
the words addressed by our Lord to St.
Paul. " My grace is sufficient for thee;
my strength is made perfect in weakness. "

It will be in companionship with humiliations, that you will be saved from falling
into sin and error, and be prepared to be

come a vessel fit for the Master's use. You will experience from time to time, a return of these humiliating states, and when you may think they have entirely passed away, they will suddenly revive. But the greater your humiliation, the more God will use you to perform his most excellent works. In this state of entire self-reduction and humiliation, your words will be clothed with power.

" I am come," says our Lord, " to bring fire on the earth." O martyr of Pure Love, — *a sacrifice* for the good of others, what if the fires be already kindled in your bosom, shrink not! If you were less to God, he might spare you.

Do not hesitate to speak to me of your sufferings, because it appears to you useless. It is not so. If you speak of them in simplicity, your heart will be relieved, and strengthened. I know how to sympathise with you. God bless you.

REPOSE OF THE SOUL IN GOD.

HAVING given up myself wholly to God, and loving Him far better than myself, how can I find any opposition to his good pleasure? How can I do otherwise than yield to one I love better than myself? How can a soul withdraw from the dominion of a Sovereign, that it loves with the whole heart? "What can separate us from the love of God, in Christ Jesus?" Although, while we remain in this life, there is a possibility of sinning, and of separation from God, and it is true, that the soul remains in oneness with Him, only by the continuance of his mercy, and that if he should leave it, it would immediately fall into sin, yet I cannot have the least fear, that my God will leave me, or that I shall ever separate myself in any degree from his love.

The creature can take no glory to itself,

to whatever state it may arrive. O that you might comprehend what I cannot express — the sense I have of the goodness of God, to keep what is his own! How jealous, how watchful he is over the soul! God seems so truly all things to me, that I seem to see nothing, to love nothing, relish nothing, only what he causes me to see, love and relish in himself. I am only capable of loving and submitting to him, so much is he my life. I believe God blindfold, without questioning or reasoning. *God is;* this is sufficient. How immense is the freedom of the soul in him! O may you not doubt, that when all of self is taken away from the creature, there remains only God. O God, can I have any self-interest, or appropriate aught as mine? In what can I take it? How strange the thought! how far removed from the possession of God! I am lost. God is.

POWER OF CASTING OUT EVIL SPIRITS.

ALTHOUGH for many years, profound truths have been revealed to me, and God has manifested his power through me, in an extraordinary manner, my state has invariably been one of infancy, simplicity and candor. God's grace has rendered me equally willing to lie concealed, or to execute his will more publicly. During seven years, without my knowing how it was accomplished, as soon as I have approached some persons, possesed by demons, the evil spirits have departed. I have realised simply a desire to relieve them, and this desire, or prayer, has been answered in a way unknown to myself. Of myself, I have no goodness nor power at all. I have only the capacity of a child — of letting myself be used by God, as pleases Him. My life appears natural. I am encompassed with infirmities. My health is greatly impaired. My infirmities are a balance-wheel, a counterpoise to exaltation. Yet life is ever flowing, without any thought of the means of sustaining it ; as we live in the air without thinking of the air we breathe.

STATE OF A SOUL RE-UNITED TO GOD.

In reply to your enquiry, my dear children, concerning my state, I would say, that exteriorly, I am open, simple, childlike. My interior resembles a drop of water, mingling and lost in the ocean, and no more discerning itself, — the sea not only surrounding, but absorbing it. In this divine immensity, the soul discerns and enjoys all objects in God. All is darkness and obscurity in respect to itself; all is light on the part of God. Thus, *God is all* to me. This has been my state more than thirty years, although in latter years I have realized greater depths in these experiences. Think of the bottomless sea ; what is thrown therein, continues sinking, without ever reaching the end. Thus divine love is the weight of the soul, that sinks it deeper and deeper in God. " God is Love, and he who dwells in love, dwells in God, and God in him." O immensity!

Jesus Christ, the embodiment of truth and love, has explained the Scriptures by fulfilling them. So when the soul has passed into God, the Word is fulfilled in the soul, as it was in Christ. O Love! thou art thyself the pure, naked, simple truth, which is expressed, not by me, but by thyself, through me. Amen.

oors, persuading the soul that this is the way to find God, and thus choking the internal process of the interior life, or, by this tension of the mind, of which I have spoken. Neither of these methods open in the soul, the interior way.

You reply, how, then, is this life accomplished? I answer, God, seeing the heart of him who seeks him within, draws near to him, and teaches him a just moderation in all things; and, by this retrenchment of all excess in externals, the soul begins to perceive the peaceful kingdom. It realizes within itself a guide, who provides for its necessities, according to divine laws, who takes away the burdens that sin imposes; a guide who does not foster corrupt nature, nor forbid innocent pleasures.

When the soul begins to perceive this kingdom, and that the King himself is manifested in some degree, it thus communes, (and we may call this the second step), O, my Beloved, I have sought thee with all the strength of my heart, in the place where thou hast taught me to seek thee, and I have there found thee! Days and nights have I passed in seeking thee. All the desires of my heart go after thee. But now I have found thee. I pray thee to reign as Sovereign, to establish thine empire in my soul. I will do thy will alone. I will resign to thee all the right I have to myself; all that thou, by thy goodness, hast given to me.

At this stage of progress, the soul ceases from self. Its work is to regard, lovingly, the operation of God, without a desire either to advance it, or place any obstacle in the way of its progress. The soul has been active, in the first stage, to destroy, with all its power, that which might hinder the kingdom of God within; and this was a great effort; for habit had rendered interior recollection very difficult, and the powers of the soul did not easily reunite themselves in one centre.

CONCISE VIEW OF THE INTERIOR WAY.

THE *soul seeks God in faith not by the reasonings of the mind and labored efforts, but by the drawings of love; to which in- clinations God responds, and instructs the soul, which co-operates actively. God then puts the soul in a passive state, where he accomplishes all, causing great progress, first by way of enjoyment, then by priva- tion, and finally by pure Love.*

What do we understand by the Interior way? It is to seek the kingdom of God within us. Luke 17, 21. We find this kingdom only where God has placed it, *within the soul.* It becomes necessary, then. to withdraw the eyes of the soul from external landmarks and observations, which man, in the pride of reason, has located around it, and rest the eye in faith, on the Word of the Lord, — " *Seek and ye shall find.*" This seeking, involves an interior activity of the soul; a desire, a determination, and searching after what is hidden.

When the soul has thus earnestly sought the kingdom of God within, this kingdom is developed little by little. Interior recollection becomes less difficult, and the presence of God more perceptible and agreeable. Formerly it was supposed, that the presence of God was only the thought of God, and that it was necessary to force the mind — to concentrate the thoughts with violence to find God. This is true in some sense, but, as the soul cannot long endure this tension, and as the kingdom of God is not found in the external vestments of the soul, but in its depths, this labor is of little avail. So little progress is made, the soul becomes discouraged, and the evil one, who fears nothing so much as the reign of God in the soul, makes an effort to draw the soul to externalities.

In order to accomplish this object, he takes two methods, either by excessive la-

Now the soul seeks no longer to combat the obstacles, which hindered its return within, but lets God combat and act in the soul. Saying, it is time O, Lord, that thou shouldst take possession of thy kingdom! Do so, I pray thee, exclusively. I desire, on my part, only to observe thine operation.

This commencement of the reign of God, and of the passive way, is very highly relished by the soul. The soul passes days, and even years, separated from creature enjoyments without weariness. It advances very much more by this way, in little time, than by all the efforts of many years. It is not without faults and imperfections, but divine love diminishes them little by little, or does not permit the soul to become disturbed by them, lest it become discouraged and its love hindered. This state is called passive love. The soul sees no cause to fear; it supposes that all the work is done, and that it has only to pass into eternity, and to enjoy this good Sovereign, who already gives himself to the soul in so much fulness.

But in the onward progress of the soul, it becomes no longer doubtful, whether the soul is to remain in the passive enjoyment of God and his communications. The soul begins to feel a drawing, to let God not only be all things in the soul, but there to reign separate from the soul's enjoyment of his gifts. The soul now experiences what is called, by the author of the Imitation of Christ, *the exile of the heart.* It hears a voice in the depth of the soul, or, rather, has an impression, that God reigns there alone. This exile is at first very painful, for it is important to notice, that, from the commencement of seeking God in the depth of the soul to the possession of him, there are many trials, temptations, sorrows. *Every successive state is marked by a purifying process.* Persons often mistake, and take the first purification for the last. When God reigns alone in the soul, separate from the action of self, and self is destroyed, it is beyond any previous state.

When the soul has ceased from its own selfish operations, and the man of sin is exterminated, its defects become more apparent, because God wishes it to comprehend what it is by itself, and what it would be without him. The soul is thus afflicted, believing it has lost the virtues, acquired with so much care, and seems to have faults that it had not before perceived. It says, with the spouse in the Canticles, "I have washed my feet, how shall I sully them?" You do not perceive, O, soul beloved, that you do not sully them in going to "open to the spouse," and that if you contract some slight impurity, he will remove it so perfectly, that you will become more beautiful. In the mean time, it is not the desire of the spouse to become beautiful in her own eyes, but to see only the beauty of her Lover. When the soul is faithful in this state, and really desires to die to itself, she is pleased only with the beauty of her Beloved, and says his beauty shall be my beauty. But it is necessary to advance beyond this, for, after being despoiled of her beauty, it would be a selfishness much greater to appropriate to herself, the beauty of her Beloved. His beauty must remain untarnished, unappropriated by her; she must leave him all, and remain in her nothing, for the nothing is her proper place. This is Perfect Love, which regards God alone.

CORRESPONDENCE BETWEEN

MADAME GUYON AND FÉNELON.

ABRIDGED.

I.

MADAME GUYON TO FÉNELON.

AGREEABLY to your kind offer, sir, to render me any assistance in your power, I take the liberty to send you some writings, which I earnestly desire you to criticise, without any regard to myself personally : spare nothing which seems to be more of self than of God. I desire only his glory. I wish, also, to ask your advice regarding the records of my life, which I have written out, during the last six years, by particular request of friends. Shall I destroy this journal, or preserve and continue it? I have not found it difficult, heretofore, to record my follies, and the mercies of God. But to continue this journal would be more difficult on account of the greater simplicity of my inward state, which is one and the same for more than eight years.

I ought to apologize, sir, for sending you the manuscripts so badly written, and otherwise so imperfect; not having re-read them. God gives me great confidence in you. I am more and more persuaded you are the person designated in my dream, eight years since.*

It is more than four years since I completed my Commentary on the Holy Scriptures. These explanations of Scripture have proceeded from a simple reading of the text. I have not had recourse to the writings of learned men. And these comments would be more perfect if I had not followed too much my own inclination, in

---

* This dream is related by Madame Guyon in her " Autobiography," vol. ii., chap 17, and is as follows : —

" I saw, in my dream, a great number of beautiful birds, which all the persons around me were eager to catch. Among them was one of extraordinary beauty, which all were bent upon pursuing. I made no effort myself, but all the birds came and offered themselves to me. They would fly away, and then return again. And, very much to my surprise, this beautiful bird came to me and did not fly away. He gave himself to me. But this beautiful bird, — beautiful above all others, — although he has not yet come to me, is not unknown. And I am certain, that, either before or after my death, he will give himself wholly to God."

continuing to write without the divine influx, not clearly discerning, at the time, my error, which I pray God those who read my writings may be able to discern.

II.

FÉNELON TO MADAME GUYON.

THE manuscripts you have sent me, madame, have afforded me great pleasure. I have found nothing in them which has not edified me very much. Be assured, I speak sincerely, and not in a complimentary way. Regarding the history of your life, I do not hesitate to say that you should not destroy it. God will draw from it fruit in its season. And the same simplicity which has enabled you, in compliance with the request of friends, to make these records, should lead you, also, to preserve and continue them from time to time, as you are able to give expression to your inward states. I am well aware, without experimental knowledge of the fact, that, the nearer one approaches to God, the more simple and uniform is his state, and the more difficult it becomes to give expression to this state. It is God alone that fills and occupies the mind.

I think you should write in simplicity and yet cautiously, in reference to individuals, and as concisely as possible; but, above all, in the liberty of the Spirit of God. Your views and explanations of Scripture have been written, I believe, according to the movement of the Spirit of God. In him, madame, I am very much devoted to your service.

III.

MADAME GUYON TO FÉNELON.

FOR several days past, sir, I have been in a state of continual prayer for you, — a state which may be compared, in its ardor and strength, to a flame which cannot be extinguished. This was the state of prayer of Jesus Christ. And it is thus the seven spirits before the throne are compared to seven lamps which burn day and night. Bear with me when I say, there yet remains in your heart some opposition to the free operation of God's Spirit; otherwise this prayer of the Spirit within me would not be so intense. I have often realized a similar state for others, but never for any one a prayer so intense and lasting. I entreat you, let the designs of God be fully accomplished in your heart and life. I believe God destines you to become a burning

and shining light to his church; and that
he wishes I should say this to you; and
that you should receive it with great simplicity, neither rejecting it by false humility, nor regarding it in any human light.
God leaves no doubt in my mind of his
holy will regarding you.

And he will use his own instruments to
accomplish his work. It is for this purpose
he is uniting me to you, in the most pure
and intimate manner; and this, notwithstanding the difference in our external cir-
cumstances, and difference in all other re-
spects. Oh, how pure, simple, divine, and
worthy of God, is communion of soul with
soul! Our blessed Lord, by his incarnation,
establishes this union. It was in this way
John was sanctified in the womb of Eliza-
beth, by the visit of Mary. It is a partici-
pation of the heavenly hierarchy, where the
blessed spirits flow together in harmony.
Oh that Christians knew their high calling
in Christ Jesus!

Let me tell you the beginnings of the way of faith differ very much from the end, or from that state when Jesus Christ, the eternal Wisdom, is revealed in the soul. And I am certain, that, after having a deep experience of the evils of your natural state, God will manifest himself to you in a remarkable manner, and set you apart for his glory.

I find myself so ill of a violent fever, that it is with difficulty I reply to your letter.

IV.

FÉNELON TO MADAME GUYON.

NOTHING moves me more sensibly, madame, than your state of ill health. And yet I cannot be troubled, because you are in the hands of God. Shall I come and see you? Neglect no means that can help you: I ask it in the name of the Lord. Your last letter will remain all my life embedded in my heart. It seems to me that our union in God is increasing. I am united to you, not only on the days of our special religious services, but on all other days. I am reading with great pleasure, and slowly, your explanations of Paul's Epistles. I have a special interest in what relates to the interior life.

I find myself often undecided in reference to small matters, — whether to do, or not to do; and have no decided choice. There are reasons on both sides. What must I do? The experience I have had, at times, in following my first movements, in which I have subsequently perceived much of selfishness, has made me hesitate to proceed in this way. And then, on the other hand, if I begin to hesitate and reason, my uncertainty increases. God humbles me. Each day I find many little things, too slight to mention, which contribute, at the moment of their occurrence, to cause me to die little by little. It is by these little matters that I discover so clearly my natural aversions, and the depths of self. But I am not hindered, voluntarily, by any of these external things. While I continue to realize many distractions, I realize also, increasingly, a sweet interior peace, and more and more of the presence of God.

If the office of bishop is conferred upon me, and I refuse it, believing I can be more useful to remain where I am than to perform the duties of a diocese, am I at liberty to follow these convictions? Pray over this matter, and please answer me, according to the light God gives you.

Shall I read your letters to Mr. C.?

I am reading slowly your commentary on the Pentateuch.

V.

MADAME GUYON TO FÉNELON.

You are so truly the Lord's, sir, and he exercises over you such watchful care, that I assure you without any hesitation, that, when it is necessary for you to decide upon any matter, God will give you, at the moment when it becomes necessary to decide, a strong inclination either to refuse or accept it, according as is his will. I am certain, that, in the present state of your heart, you are not hindered from following God's will by any voluntary movement. Involuntary distractions, when one is not hindered by them, by making too much account of them, purify the soul; and the knowledge of them will prepare the soul for another state, which is yet, with you, afar off, — a state of purity, without any distractions; a state where all the powers of the soul are reduced to unity; in which state the mind and heart make only one act.

Your prayer is less easy, because God, wishing to become your principle, takes away your own thoughts, in order to substitute what is more in accordance with his will. God is leading you, not by the way of great crosses and violent conflicts, but by the way of littleness. You cannot become too little, too childlike; and therefore God has chosen a child to be your companion, to teach you the route of little children. When you reach this state of littleness, God will renew within you his image: you will live no more. Jesus Christ will live in you.

To accomplish this is the work of the Holy Spirit. He will send the devouring fire before his face; that is, he will send his Spirit before his word, in order that the Spirit burn and destroy all that is evil: and then Jesus Christ the Word will be formed in you; you will be changed into his image, from glory to glory. "Our God is a consuming fire."

I cannot now speak of this new life in Christ, which will be of infinite extent. Suffice to say, you will know all things. It is to this blessed life, which is reached only by the death of self, that I invite you.

Do not read at present the whole of the Pentateuch, but only that portion of it which relates to the passage of the Israelites across the Red Sea into the Promised Land.

VI.

FÉNELON TO MADAME GUYON.

I FIND myself willing all, and willing
nothing; that is, I will all that God wills,
and will nothing of myself. My will, as it
seems to me, is fixed in this state. And
yet I find my natural aversions and inclinations pushing out, on all sides, like the
leaves of the tree in springtime. I am as
a garrison besieged, the walls all broken
down. I cannot conceal this state of desolation from my friends: it is apparent in
my countenance, and in the tones of my
voice. And yet I have no great temptations. It is only my weakness that makes
the temptations strong. I have a disincli-
nation to the place of prayer; and, when
there. my temptations are great: I do not
find that inward recollection and enjoyment of God I anticipated; and, it seems to

me, I accomplish nothing. In the depths of my being, I find a repose in God; but, in the business of the day, there is less recollection or perception of God. I am sometimes tempted to hasten matters; to outstrip myself, and get beyond this state: but I content myself to leave to each moment all its distractions. My soul is so barren, and I am so much occupied in external duties, that it seems to me, sometimes, as if there was no place for God in my heart. The distress I realize on account of my low state; and my desire to be wholly the Lord's alone sustains me.

I am satisfied, from present experience, that the enjoyment of repose, and the occupation of the soul, in this way, is a return of selfishness very dangerous. And thus the soul is retarded by the same means that was helpful in a previous stage of progress. I understand that means are to be used only as a proof of our fidelity and subjection to God, and not as real supports to the soul. Relish of retirement is a state of which God becomes jealous, after having made use of this means to draw us from ourselves. Unhappy he who amuses himself with the gifts of grace, as the natural man with the endowments of Nature. Wisdom, too human, becomes a snare. I cannot find in it either peace or despoilment : it is a heavy clog to my steps

VII.

MADAME GUYON TO FÉNELON.

THE point of consideration most important for you, sir, is the loss of your own will in the will of God. God desires to lead you himself; and all he requires of you is to permit him to do so. And, in order to this, you must suffer yourself to die daily, and moment by moment, by means of all the passing events of life: suffering your repugnances to be consumed in you, by not regarding them, let them suffer and die.

The way of pure faith, in the loss of the will, is so barren to Nature, that the soul sees nothing, and holds to nothing seemingly. But often, when one prop is removed, the soul finds itself clinging to another. And at this point, letting go the hold of some things, the will awakens even to a firmer grasp of some other things.

Aside from the usual way in which God leads souls, there is a specific leading, appropriate to the state and character of each one. And I have never known two persons so near alike as to be led precisely in the same way. And these diversities, giving to each one an individual character, and leading adapted to that character, redound to the glory of God. What might cause the death of another might not answer for you, on account of the greater depth of your interior. The suffering of advancing souls arises from resistance to God's will, although this will may not always be understood at the time. This resistance, however innocent, causes a disturbed state of the soul.

We must not judge of the propriety of God's dealings with us by our relish or disrelish of these dealings. He who has lost his own will is so well balanced as to be easily moved by God, when the right moment comes for a decision. The perfect will of God, by which the soul is introduced to its first principle, and to the consummation of unity in God, although very certain in itself, leaves the soul, in its incipient state of progress, to a thousand uncertainties. Certainty would be a prop, and hinder the loss of the will.

You may not be able, at present, to understand what is meant by the loss of the will. Nor is it easy to give expression to a state so exalted, and implying such union with God. "The Torrents" * is well adapted to persons in all stages of progress.

The more resolute and fixed your will becomes, the greater your sensibility to natural aversions and faults, because of the increased opposition of the will to all that is evil. But be encouraged: it is as a tree, which, dying at its stock, is pushing out only false buds, which serve only to

* "The Torrents," by Madame Guyon, translated from the French by Rev. Mr. Ford.

consume its sap, and hasten its death. As you reach the state of death, which is preceded by an experience of your misery and poverty, great truths will be discovered to you, known only to those who are taught of God. Then you will know God alone is truth.

Oh that I could express to you what I now perceive of the designs of God, in giving you his spirit of truth, which searches you out, and leaves you in possession of nothing in order to possess you himself! Leave yourself, then, all empty, as you are, with God; and consider yourself the happiest of men, because the most feeble. God designs to make you the father of a great people, — a people peculiar, humble, docile, childlike; and, on this account, he will lay deep the foundation of your spiritual edifice. By the loss of all things you will obtain infinite riches, infinite freedom. You will be constrained to say with Paul (2 Cor. xii. 10), " Therefore I take pleasure in infirmities, in reproaches, in necessities, in persecutions, in distresses, for Christ's sake; for when I am weak, then am I strong."

VIII.

FÉNELON TO MADAME GUYON.

I AM quite certain, madame, that none can comprehend the state of pure love, except those who have experienced it. No one knows the depths of the Spirit of God, but the Spirit itself. He, therefore, who has no experience of this state judges imperfectly, according to his limited view. It is on this account I am silent, and am willing to wait until it pleases God to give me a clear knowledge or experience of this state. I understand the state of death which St. Paul depicts, expressed by these words, "It is no more I that live, but Jesus Christ in me," to be a state in which one is crucified to the world, that is, to all that is not God; a state in which one feels no condemnation, without, at the same time, possessing any righteousness of his own;

a state in which one glories only in the
Lord, and speaks of himself as of another,
and fears not to say of himself, or of the
grace of God in him, sublime things, because such an one is out of self, dwelling
in God, and God in him. When one has
reached this state, the death of self is consummated, but life is not. This life of God
in the soul increases from day to day, and
will be increasing through all eternity.
In this state, righteousness is not only im-
puted, but really possessed by the soul,
by the indwelling of the spirit of God.
These are my views on an experience or
state I have not yet reached. But, as I
view it, no one is infallible, although dead
to the selfish life. The faults committed
in this state are involuntary, ordinarily,
and not those of actual disobedience to
God's known will.

Yesterday I committed a trespass against
a person who is by nature very disagreeable
to me. This fault humbled, although it did

not distress me. I propose to visit him this morning, to make suitable reparation for the wrong.

Every day, I see my faults ; and I am quite certain that self is not dead. I realize movements so natural and so evil, that I must conclude the poison is within, and will not leave me without a violent operation. At times, I find it necessary to amuse myself in various ways, as a child plays. There is a little child here, two and a half years old, with whom I play sometimes.

Nothing affords me so much pleasure as the thought that I am united to you in God.

IX.

MADAME GUYON TO FÉNELON.

I HAVE recently, sir, seen clearly, in the light of God, the origin and nature of spiritual unions, — the mutual dependence of one soul upon another, and the results of union. Oh, how beautiful are our advancing steps in the clearer light of God! The soul, being created originally in the image of God, and being restored to this image by means of the personal incarnation of the Word, receives a part of his divine nature or attributes. In receiving a part of this nature, the soul receives the quality of productiveness, or power of communicating grace. It is thus in union with God; and, being made a partaker of the nature of God, that soul unites itself to soul, and in this way communicates grace, as God communicates himself, his essence and nature and power, to his creatures. The soul being in God and of God, it draws and penetrates other souls, by means of the divine operation through this soul, as an absorbing and reflecting medium. Although those intervening rays may seem of themselves to draw others, it is God alone who acts as first cause. It is not easy to separate the ray from the body of the sun, although it is distinct. And those souls who are nearest to God, or in closest union with him, possess the most of this power. Yes: it is God alone who draws and unites souls in himself to one another; the intervening soul presenting no obstacle, on account of its purity and transparency, but serving rather as a medium for the communication of grace. It is thus one soul bears the burden of another soul. It is in this way God has caused me to suffer on your account. In advancing to this state of union, the soul will encounter whirlwinds of temptation, but the truth of God will stand. The vessel, although beaten by the winds and waves, will assuredly reach a safe harbor. God is pilot.

I have found it difficult to give expression to this experience. May your light supply what is lacking. Have the goodness to express to me your views, even if opposed to my own.

Please read fifty-fourth chapter of Isaiah, and give me your views of it. I have opened the Bible several times of late to this chapter, and God has given me an understanding of it adapted to my state. The grace that God gives me to aid souls is increasing, and the number of such persons is increasing. The results are wonderful. I remain with you, ever the same, one in God.

X.

FÉNELON TO MADAME GUYON.

SINCE yesterday, I have desired to write you, madame, although I had resolved not to do so before seeing you, which, I trust, will be soon. I often think of you, and find myself more and more united to you in God. I am one with you in the Infinite, and it seems to me we shall remain always one in him. I am as confident as you are, that God blesses me through you. My thoughts of you are always blessed, because I never see you out of God, and see God through you, without resting at all in you. Sometimes I experience some little doubts and temptations regarding this state; but they quickly vanish, having no real foundation. Our union is established, and at the same time increasing. I agree with you, there are no unions so blessed as the union of souls in God, although I can give no very definite expression of this state of union. I could not speak of any one particular thought I have of you, although I think of you so often. It is a general view or impression of you, accompanied with great peace and enjoyment in God. My confidence in you is unbounded, on account of your goodness, your simplicity, your knowledge and experience of the deep things of God, and, finally, on account of the designs of God in relation to myself through you.

I have read twice the fifty-fourth chapter of Isaiah. It represents the glory and fruitfulness of the Church of Christ, which is at first as the barren and forsaken spouse. Souls whom God destines to draw other souls to himself pass at first through the wilderness state, stripped of the all of self, which is a way full of tribulation to the natural heart. But subsequently, when the soul is prepared, God enriches

her and renders her fruitful in himself.
Thus it is with you. I am not able to
speak of what you are to others, but I
know what you are to me. I shall be most
happy to see you soon, and to sit with you
in prayerful recollection before God.

Be persuaded I write you in whole-
hearted simplicity. You know with what
grateful recollections I am yours in our
Lord.

XI.

MADAME GUYON TO FÉNELON.

You have explained, sir, in few words, the nature of the union of souls in God, — a union existing in great simplicity of state, a union in which is no space or nothing separating, because it is established of God and is in God. I find you in God, and God in you. The greater my union with God, the greater my union with you. I realize, at times, a more perceptible overflowing and drawing of your soul with mine into the fulness of God, and yet in the same purity and simplicity.

I am not surprised that doubts sometimes arise in your mind concerning this state. It is so with myself; but they vanish in the thought that God takes pleasure to glorify himself in his children, even the weakest. And, besides this, I have a cer-

MADAME GUYON TO FÉNELON.

tain indifference to all that relates to me
personally. I desire, first of all, the glory
of God, whatever becomes of me. Only
yesterday, I was questioning if I had not
of myself induced this state; and I asked
the Lord, if it was his Spirit that was op-
erating through me on other souls, that a
person who was then present might experience the results of this operation. And
immediately this person, who was entirely
ignorant of my prayer, experienced a sensible communication of grace, and spoke to
me of the great peace and enjoyment of
God which had just been imparted to
her soul. It has been impressed on my
mind for several days past, that the love of
God for his creatures goes out of himself
like a torrent, and blesses all hearts open
to receive it; and that the love which the
holy soul experiences and diffuses is only
a portion of this same love.

Yesterday I had a strong impression (I
was sick in bed) that I was called to bear

the cross of Christ to a still greater degree than ever before. All I could do was to say, "Let thy will, O God! be accomplished in me." And in thus surrendering myself anew, to bear all sufferings in union with my Lord, and for the good of his church, these words were given me: "I will espouse thee to me forever; yea, I will betroth thee unto me, in righteousness, and in loving kindness, and in mercies" (Hosea ii. 19, 20).

Notwithstanding my presentiment that I should not die very soon, I was so ill yesterday, I thought my end was near. In the evening, I had a strong conviction that I should recover; and, with this conviction, I experienced such a fulness of God's Spirit, and such enlargement of heart, as greatly to increase my physical strength. But I can speak to no persons here of these peculiar exercises. I know it is not best to see you too frequently, and I know our Lord can supply the lack of personal interviews; and even now, while I am writing, I find my soul so united to you as to make me realize that no distance or space in the natural world can interrupt the intercourse of souls made one in God.

I am, in him, all to you he makes me to be.

XII.

MADAME GUYON TO FÉNELON.

LAST night, sir, for the first time since our acquaintance, I had a very singular dream of you. You will smile at my simplicity in relating it; but no matter: you will yet become as much of a child as I am; and it is only little children that can enter into the kingdom of heaven.

I saw in my dream a very deep valley. You were on the summit of the mountain, and about to descend. There were a few persons present, who had with great difficulty ascended the mountain, which we were to descend. You and I were seated together, and were gliding along down the summit, without any movement of our own. This descent of the valley, or declivity, was marked with deep furrows, or ridges, at regular intervals, which made it easier to ascend the mountain, but seemed to present an obstacle to our descending in the manner in which we were seated, making no movement ourselves. But this apparent difficulty was obviated by the flexibility of the mountain, which seemed to abase itself in these ridges, as the waves of the sea; so that we descended easily, carried along by the movement of the mountain.

One of tne persons who had ascended the mountain — a woman — stopped you, and, while she was conversing with you, hindered you from descending, and hindered, also, the movement of the mountain. I was arrested with you, and understood, that, as I was descending only on your account, I should be retarded as long as you were. While you were being arrested, I suffered much. When this woman withdrew, I was more strongly bound to you than ever; and our inclination was mutual. I said to you, " O my child! how much I have suffered, while you have been hindered by this woman!" You replied, " I, too, have suffered much; for I was removed from my right position, and where my inclination led me; but I am taught a lesson : *to let nothing hinder me.*" After this, we descended very rapidly, and with great delight, and repose of soul in soul. We found ourselves, unawares, in a room at the base of the mountain, where were also a few persons of great innocence and purity, like ourselves. I said to you, " The liberty which you have given me to call you ' *My child* ' pleases me, and removes from me the restraint that I have hitherto experienced." Here is my dream. It seems very clear to me. I will leave you to penetrate its depths.

XIII.

FÉNELON TO MADAME GUYON.

I READ with pleasure, madame, all that comes from your pen, and pray that you may follow freely the inclination God gives you to write me ; and, be assured, I shall be very much edified. I am so in advance, by a cordial reception of all. I am willing you should make reserves of what is beyond my depth; but I pray you to make no reserves as to what I need, and, especially, to reduce me to the simplicity of a child. God has given you an understanding of your dream. Please enlighten me. I perceive readily that human wisdom, personified by the woman, is a great hinderance to my progress. Does this relate to the past, or to the present time ? Am I now in the state in which you are arrested by me? What do you understand by the room at the base of the mountain? Please express to me unreservedly your thoughts on the dream.

If you know any point in which I fail, any one thing which hinders the free opera- tion of God's Spirit, I entreat you to tell me plainly, without any reserve; for I desire only the accomplishment of God's will: all else is nothing to me. I know well that my wisdom must die; but all I can do is to hold myself in the crucible. God must strike the blow. I accept all that God orders, without any self-reserves. What more can I do? Will you do the rest for me by your prayers? I am willing to pro- gress as fast or as slowly as God pleases, whatever it may cost me. I count as noth- ing all the sufferings I may endure. "Suffi- cient unto the day is the evil thereof." He who permits the evil will bring good out of the evil. Besides, I would not think of good relative to myself; for I desire to lose sight of myself, in order that God's will may be fully accomplished. I would not have you suffer on my account. I am feeble both in mind and body, and unfitted for my external duties. But my soul rests in God. I take time for rest and recreation, and amuse myself as well as I can. My seasons of prayer are irregular, and partake rather of silent meditation than of petition. My prayer is most natural when riding or walking. When I take a fixed position, my thoughts wander. You can judge from this expression of my feelings how humiliating is my experience. You know, as well as myself, what God permits me to be to you.

Books on the Deeper Christian Life

Each year we publish a catalogue that lists and describes the books we publish. If you would like this catalogue please write for it. The books - and prices - listed below are as of 1983, and are subject to change at any time.

You may order these books directly or from your favorite Christian bookstore.

Books by Madame Guyon

Guyon's Spiritual Letters	6.95
Song of Songs	5.95
Union With God	4.95
Experiencing the Depths	4.95
Genesis	5.95

The Library of Spiritual Classics

Fenelon's Spiritual Letters	4.95
Divine Life (Mary McDonough)	5.95
The Spiritual Guide (Michael Molinos)	5.95
Practicing His Presence (Lawrence)	4.95

Other Books

The Inward Journey (Gene Edwards)	5.95
A Tale of Three Kings (Gene Edwards)	4.95
Torch of the Testimony (John W. Kennedy)	6.95
The Early Church (Gene Edwards)	4.95
Letters to a Devastated Christian (Gene Edwards)	3.95

Coming in 1984

The Divine Romance
Foundation Stones
Our Mission

Christian Books: Box 959 Augusta, Maine 04330